THOMAS JEFFERSON
VERSUS
RELIGIOUS OPPRESSION

THOMAS JEFFERSON
VERSUS
RELIGIOUS
OPPRESSION

By
Frank Swancara

UNIVERSITY BOOKS • NEW YORK

CONTENTS

THOMAS JEFFERSON'S BILL
FOR ESTABLISHING
RELIGIOUS FREEDOM

Well aware that the opinions and belief of men depend not on their own will, but follow involuntarily the evidence proposed to their minds; that[1] Almighty God hath created the mind free, *and manifested his supreme will that free it shall remain by making it altogether insusceptible of restraint;* that all attempts to influence it by temporal punishments, or burthens, or by civil incapacitations, tend only to beget habits of hypocrisy and meanness, and are a departure from the plan of the holy author of our religion, who being lord both of body and mind, yet chose not to propagate it by coercions on either, as was in his Almighty power to do, *but to extend it by its influence on reason alone;* that the impious presumption of legislators and rulers, civil as well as ecclesiastical, who, being themselves but fallible and uninspired men, have assumed dominion over the faith of others, setting up their own opinions and modes of thinking as the only true and infallible, and as such endeavoring to impose them on others, hath established and maintained false religions over the greatest part of the world and through all time: That to compel a man to furnish contributions of money for the propagation of opinions which he disbelieves *and abhors,* is sinful and tyrannical; that even the forcing him to support this or that teacher of his own religious persuasion, is depriving him of the comfortable liberty of giving his contributions to the particular pastor whose morals he would make his pattern, and whose powers he feels most persuasive to righteousness; and is withdrawing from the ministry those

---

[1] Italicized words and phrases were deleted in the statute as passed by the Virginia Assembly.

temporary rewards, which proceeding from an approbation of their personal conduct, are an additional incitement to earnest and unremitting labours for the instruction of mankind; that our civil rights have no dependance on our religious opinions, any more than our opinions in physics or geometry; that therefore the proscribing any citizen as unworthy the public confidence by laying upon him an incapacity of being called to offices of trust and emolument, unless he profess or renounce this or that religious opinion, is depriving him injuriously of those privileges and advantages to which, in common with his fellow citizens, he has a natural right; that it tends also to corrupt the principles of that *very* religion it is meant to encourage, by bribing, with a monopoly of worldly honours and emoluments, those who will externally profess and conform to it; that though indeed these are criminal who do not withstand such temptation, yet neither are those innocent who lay the bait in their way; *that the opinions of men are not the object of civil government, nor under its jurisdiction;* that to suffer the civil magistrate to intrude his powers into the field of opinion and to restrain the profession or propagation of principles on supposition of their ill tendency is a dangerous fallacy, which at once destroys all religious liberty, because he being of course judge of that tendency will make his opinions the rule of judgment, and approve or condemn the sentiments of others only as they shall square with or differ from his own; that it is time enough for the rightful purposes of civil government for its officers to interfere when principles break out into overt acts against peace and good order; and finally, that truth is great and will prevail if left to herself; that she is the proper and sufficient antagonist to error, and has nothing to fear from the conflict unless by human interposition disarmed of her natural weapons, free argument and debate; errors ceasing to be dangerous when it is permitted freely to contradict them.

WE THE GENERAL ASSEMBLY OF VIRGINIA DO ENACT that no man shall be compelled to frequent or support any religious worship, place, or ministry whatsoever, nor shall be enforced, restrained, molested, or burthened in his body or goods, nor shall otherwise suffer, on account of his religious opinions or belief; but that all men shall be free to profess, and by argument to maintain, their opinions in matters of religion, and that the same shall in no wise diminish, enlarge, or affect their civil capacities.

And though we well know that this Assembly, elected by the people for the ordinary purposes of legislation only, have no power to restrain the acts of succeeding Assemblies, constituted with powers equal to our own, and that therefore to declare this act irrevocable would be of no effect in law; yet we are free to declare, and do declare, that the rights hereby asserted are of the natural rights of mankind, and that if any act shall be hereafter passed to repeal the present or to narrow its operation, such act will be an infringement of natural right.

PREFACE

This author's writings began in 1908 when as a stenographer in a law office he chanced to see a digest of judicial decisions which held a person to be incompetent as a witness if he not believe in *divine* punishments. Under such case law Clarence Darrow would have been disqualified. Thereafter "witness" cases were examined, and in 1932 *The Virginia Law Review* published the contribution entitled *Iniquity in the Name of Justice*. It was reprinted in *Lawyer and Banker*. Other articles followed. Some are listed in the author index to the 1934 Supplement to *Wigmore on Evidence*.

In 1936 a local printer published a collection of articles by this author in a book entitled *Obstruction of Justice by Religion*. It shared its author's obscurity, but was accepted by a few university libraries.

In 1948 came the *McCollum* decision, which provoked a contributor to the *American Bar Association Journal* to use these words: "The court which . . . handed down the infamous McCollum decision . . . and played the Communist game." That language and other attacks on the decision induced the writing of *Separation of Religion and Government* (1950). A brief review of it appeared in the July, 1951, *William and Mary Quarterly*. The title of the 1950 book was derived from James Madison's *Detached Memoranda*, which contained the expression: "Strongly guarded as is the separation between Religion and Government in the Constitution of the United States. . . ."

Of course, each failure to interest a publisher in the present work induced a rewriting of one or more pages, the physical and mental exertion sometimes encouraged by remembering that Lord Brougham wrote and rewrote parts of his argument in Queen Caroline's case seventeen times. Countless paragraphs in this book were made as short as possible so as to encourage a reader not to stop, and also because of lack of easy access to law reports and Howell's *State Trials*, where additional relevant material would appear. And a detailed and thoroughly comprehensive work would be enormous. The report of one trial alone, as that of Kneeland in *American State Trials*, took about a hundred pages.

Naturally the writer consulted Henry S. Randall's *The Life of Thomas Jefferson*. The biographer there said that Count de Volney "stained his fame by productions of the rankest atheism." It was surprising, therefore, to find that in 1924 Gilbert Chinard published, in French, the Jefferson-Volney correspondence, which showed that Jefferson had translated Volney's *Ruins of Empires* from the beginning to the end of the twentieth chapter. The fact of such translation is today stated on library index cards relating to that book.

The libraries are replete with "Jefferson" books, but not one of them, except Dr. Julian P. Boyd's *Papers*, shows what words, phrases, and clauses were stricken from Jefferson's Bill before its passage, in his absence, in 1786. Such deleted parts are set forth in this book. They were unknown to, and therefore not mentioned by, the clerics who assailed Jefferson in 1800 and later.

In 1953 the Library of Congress issued *A Catalogue of the Library of Thomas Jefferson*. It contains the titles of Jefferson's books—some of an atheistic or deistic tenor—and extracts from correspondence he had with donors or vendors of them. His notes appear on the margins of some, one being on a page of Priestley's *An History of the Early Opinions concerning Jesus Christ*. Jefferson there comments on the refusal of a cleric to admit the forgery of I John V, 7 as then worded in the King James version.

The *Catalogue* is used by this writer in connection with a second, and different, Jefferson book, but for present purposes the *Catalogue* was useful in showing that Jefferson had possession of the first four volumes of *State Trials*. These volumes reported trials prior to 1727, some of which were prosecutions for some kind of nonconformity in matters of religion. This writer had access only to Howell's *State Trials*, which in Volume V reports Nayler's case of 1656, and in Volume VI the trial of Benjamin Keach, Baptist. The trial and hanging of the boy Thomas Aikenhead are described in Volume XIII. From some source Jefferson learned of the trial of John Asgill, for the *Catalogue* shows his possession of *John Asgill's Defence upon His Expulsion from the House of Commons in 1707.*

Howell's *State Trials*, thirty-six volumes, was found, consulted, and often cited by Theodore Schroeder in *Constitutional Free Speech* (1919) which devotes its 456 pages to the *un*constitutionality of "blasphemy" statutes and decisions. Schroeder quotes Justice William Jay on the free speech clause in the 1821 Constitution of New York. Jay's instruction to a Grand Jury contained the words: "Hence, infidels and Christians, and politicians of every name and character, have an equal and undoubted right to publish their sentiments, and to endeavor to make converts to them." To the same effect was a long note to an American 1803 edition of Blackstone, the note being written by Professor St. George Tucker, who later held high judgeships. The chapter on Blasphemy laws and prosecutions hereinafter omits much of Schroeder's material, to avoid undue length and repetitions.

Conducting a research in history or biography leads to surprises in matters not relevant to the project being pursued. After finding that Jefferson, in some note, approvingly cited Chillingworth, it was accidentally discovered that Lord Chesterfield, too, thought well of the English divine, for the *Letter* of February 7, 1749, included:

The herd of mankind can hardly be said to think; their

notions are almost all adoptive. . . . The good Protestant conviction, that the Pope is both Antichrist and the Whore of
Babylon, is a more effectual preservative, in this country,
against popery, than all the solid and unanswerable arguments
of Chillingworth.

A further surprise is that Chillingworth's worst enemy was
not a papist but the Puritan preacher Francis Cheynell who,
at Chillingworth's funeral (1644), flung a copy of *Religion
of Protestants* into the grave to "rot with its author and see
corruption."

When burnings for heresy stopped, burnings of books did
not; and the sentence pronounced against Benjamin Keach,
author of a Baptist primer, included this: "And there [at the
pillory] your book shall be openly burnt before your face,
. . . in disgrace of you and your doctrine." Even Jefferson's
favorite book, Priestley's *An History of the Corruptions of
Christianity* (1782) did not escape the fate of being burned
by the town hangman at Dordrecht, Holland. The Jefferson
library contained Charles Blount's *Anima Mundi* (1679),
and the article in *Encyclopedia Britannica* (eleventh edition,
4:87) says: "It was suppressed by order of the bishop of
London, and even burnt by some over-zealous official, . . ."

Jefferson was a book *saver*, not burner, as when preserving,
from the library of John Wales, a deistic work by Thomas
Chubb (1679–1746). Or when keeping, from the library of
Benjamin Franklin, a copy of *Letter from Thrasbyulus to
Leucippus.*

The opinion of the Massachusetts judges in the Quaker-
hanging case is of book length. Hence the brevity of quotations from it in the chapter hereinafter on persecutions of
Quakers. To reduce cost of printing, and to minimize a
reader's mental labor, such abridgments are many. Judges
often delivered verbose opinions to show conformity to popular prejudices when imposing a penalty or an incapacitation
upon a person admitting nonbelief of some notorious dogma

of the major sects. If interested, a reader may find the opinions in their entirety in the law reports. Many would show the aptness of Jefferson's phrase: ". . . judges accomplices in the frauds of the clergy."

This book is the one that for the first time *directly* calls attention to Jefferson's Preamble in the Bill as worded when first introduced, in 1779. Many words and phrases of secular significance were expunged by the Virginia Assembly by divided votes.

The many campus demonstrations of recent times raise an inference that the younger generation perceives and abhors tyranny by the authorities. In the past the minors thoughtlessly acquiesced in whatever their elders made conventional, including disregard of sufferings by the lowly or obscure. When judges in murder trials rejected dying declarations of victims, solely because the latter did not believe in a Jehovah, the public remained apathetic. The reformer or humanitarian, such as Upton Sinclair, was a rare human being, and not young. Historians who feelingly wrote of medieval cruelties, as Thomas B. Macaulay did on the trial and execution of young Thomas Aikenhead, were elderly men. This book is therefore dedicated to students everywhere who perceive and resent injustice and oppose authoritative "brutality" when and wherever it shows its fangs.

Chapter One

INTRODUCTION

The inscription of Thomas Jefferson's monument bears the lines:

**AUTHOR OF THE DECLARATION OF INDEPEN-
DENCE, OF THE STATUTE OF VIRGINIA FOR
RELIGIOUS FREEDOM, AND FATHER OF THE
UNIVERSITY OF VIRGINIA**

As if to provide a cushion from clerical censures, the Statute of Virginia is placed typographically between the lines relating to the universally approbated Declaration of Independence and the University. Notwithstanding that it was "for religious freedom," some clergymen perceived the scope of the clause: ". . . that all men shall be free to profess, and by argument to maintain, their opinions in matters of religion."

That language would preclude or end all statutory and common law disabilities and penalties for avowal or advocacy of heretical or unbelieving opinions about the Bible or "in matters of religion." The civil disabilities at common law will be specified in Chapter X.

In 1836 a religious historian denounced the Statute as "an alliance between civil authority and infidelity, . . . ruinous in its results."[1] The term "infidelity" was often used, and meant nonbelief of inspiration and inerrancy of biblical narratives of miracles and of divine interventions in human affairs. For being anti-Trinitarians, deists and Unitarians were deemed to be "infidels."

Jefferson's Bill was replete with the word "opinions," but the term "faith" appeared only once, in the phrase "faith of

15

others." Why he would remove penalties for having or avowing "opinions" is indicated by the first line of his Bill as first written, and deleted by the Assembly, to the effect that opinions are involuntary. On that point Robert G. Ingersoll wrote:

> The brain thinks without asking our consent. We believe, or we disbelieve, without an effort of the will. Belief is a result. It is the effect of evidence upon the mind. The scales turn in spite of him who watches. There is no opportunity of being honest, or dishonest, in the formation of an opinion. The conclusion is entirely independent of desire.

Consistent with Jefferson's phraseology is Section 40, Article IV, of the Constitution of Michigan:

> The Legislature shall not diminish or enlarge the civil or political rights, privileges and capacities of any person on account of his *opinion* or belief concerning matters of religion.

The phrase "for religious freedom" conformed to public opinion and tended to preclude critical attention to the clause providing that "opinions in matters of religion . . . shall in no wise *diminish* . . . or affect . . . civil capacities." That favored the unbelievers who had "opinions" instead of the Christian "faith." They were also favored by the clause having the words "by *argument* to maintain . . . opinions. . . ." Secularism could be promoted or defended by "argument." It was more effective against orthodoxy than were the higher mathematics denounced by Bishop George Berkeley (1685-1753) "as leading to freethinking."[2]

For centuries it was a crime "by argument to maintain" heterodox opinions in theological matters. Because governments proscribed argument and imposed the civil disabilities, Jefferson wrote in the Preamble to the Bill "that the opinions of men are not the object of civil government, nor under its jurisdiction." In *Notes on Virginia* he reaffirmed that principle when he wrote:

> The legislative powers of government extend to such acts only as are injurious to others. It does me no injury for my neighbor to say there are 20 gods, or no God. It neither picks my pocket nor breaks my leg.

Referring to that paragraph, the Reverend John M. Mason wrote:

> . . . this is the morality of devils, which would break in an instant every link in the chain of human friendship, and transform the globe into one equal scene of desolation and horror, where fiend would prowl with fiend for plunder and blood; yet Atheism "neither picks my pocket nor breaks my leg." . . .[3]

So it was meant that "Atheism," if prevalent, would create fiends that "would prowl . . . for plunder and blood."

Years before, Lamettrie in Holland had written to show that, in his words, "Atheism is the only means of ensuring the happiness of the world, which has been rendered impossible by the wars brought about by theologians." For his thesis Lamettrie was compelled to quit Holland. Frederick the Great then gave him shelter, protection, and a position at court in Berlin.[4]

The Reverend Mason in his notorious pamphlet of 1800 assailed Frederick also, declaring that the latter "was one of the knot of conspirators who, with Voltaire at their head, plotted the extermination of Christianity. . . ."

On May 26, 1800, without naming the calumniators, Jefferson wrote to James Monroe: ". . . as to the calumny of atheism, I am so broken to calumnies of every kind . . . that I entirely disregard it. . . ."[5]

Twenty-three years later he had occasion to say:

Fanaticism, it is true, is not sparing of her invectives against those who refuse blindly to follow her dictates in abandonment of their own reason. Yet why retort with invectives? It is better always to set a good example than to follow a bad one.[6]

Jefferson noted that others had suffered the "calumny of atheism," once writing that the atheists Diderot, d'Alembert, d'Holbach, and Condorcet "are known to have been the most virtuous of men . . . their virtue, then, must have had some other foundation than the love of God."[7] What the foundation could have been may be inferred from Jefferson's letter of August 10, 1787, to Peter Carr:

Fix Reason firmly in her seat. . . . If it ends in a belief that there is no God, you will find incitements to virtue in the comfort and pleasantness you will feel in its exercise, and the love of others which it will procure you.[8]

There was no danger that Carr would become a "fiend" as defined by the Reverend Mason.

To avoid "calumny" or prosecution, atheists, deists, Unitarians, and other heterodox persons generally refrained from disclosure of their opinions. In 1812 Daniel Isaac Eaton published a Paine essay, was prosecuted, and at the trial argued much like Priestley did in books which Jefferson extolled. How the judge and the prosecutor treated Eaton and his arguments is the subject of Chapter II. Other prosecutions are treated in Chapter VI.

Because the Statute precluded such prosecutions in Virginia, and was a precursor to future reforms elsewhere, Jefferson on December 16, 1786, soon after its passage, wrote to James Madison:

. . . it is comfortable to see the standard of reason at length erected, after so many ages during which the human mind has

been held in vassalage by kings, priests & nobles; and it is hon-
orable for us to have produced the first legislature who had
the courage to declare that the reason of man may be trusted
with the formation of his own opinions.[9]

And this to George Wythe on August 13, 1786:

. . . If all the sovereigns of Europe were to set themselves
to work to emancipate the minds of their subjects from their
present ignorance & prejudices & that as zealously as they now
endeavor the contrary, a thousand years would not place them
on that high ground on which our common people are now
setting out.[10]

Before the American Revolution, history was so replete
with ecclesiastical cruelties, forgeries, and frauds that, as a
student thereof and a humanitarian, Jefferson was bound to
vow "eternal hostility against every form of tyranny over
the mind." The common people, called "the vulgar," had
been coerced into real or pretended conformity and orthodoxy, which Jefferson noticed when writing:

What has been the effect of coercion? To make one half
the world fools, and the other half hypocrites; to support
roguery and error all over the earth.

Those refusing to be either "fools" or "hypocrites" suffered
enough to remind Robert Burns of "man's inhumanity to
man."
One of many forms of "coercion" was the imposition of
civil disabilities even for unexpressed heterodoxy, as where
a Tennessee judge held that the Tennessee Constitution
barred an atheist from being a juror "because he cannot be
trusted."[11]
Some notice of ecclesiastical exploitations of poverty, cre-
dulity, and ignorance is taken in Chapter V, which has

subdivisions also on persecutions of Quakers and Baptists.

Jefferson noticed that in Locke's *Letter Concerning Toleration* it was written: "Lastly, those are *not* at all to be tolerated who deny the being of a God." This explains Jefferson's note, ending with: ". . . but where he [Locke] stopped short, we may go on."[12] The "go on" doctrine was paraphrased by Mr. Justice Jackson in 1952, when he said:

> The day that this country ceases to be free for irreligion, it will cease to be free for religion, except for the sect that can win political power.[13]

Mr. Justice Black, in the same case, added:

> State help to religion injects political and party prejudice into a holy field. It too often substitutes force for prayer, and persecution for persuasion. Government should not be allowed, under cover of the soft euphemism of "co-operation," to steal into the sacred area of religious choice.

There is generally some *hate* on the part of those who injure a citizen on account of his nonacceptance of some article of their faith, which fact may have prompted Justice Holmes to use the expression: ". . . not free thought for those who agree with us, but freedom for the thought that we hate."[14]

Prior to the respectability gained by Unitarians, humanists, and the silently indifferent, the heterodox citizen was by the orthodox conformer called, with aspersive intent, an "infidel." The predominant sects would cause the civil government to persecute the "unbeliever" in the various ways indicated by the Table of Contents of this book. At first, judges participated willingly, but later they continued so to do under pretense of compulsion of *stare decisis*, *i.e.*, taking earlier decisions as imperative authority, sometimes with an exordium such as this:

Ours is a religious people. This is historically true. American life everywhere, as expressed by its laws, its business, its customs, its society, gives abundant recognition and proof of the fact.[15]

To make that statement seem, or be, more authoritative, they cite *Church of Holy Trinity v. United States*, 143 U.S. 457.

Chapter Two

UNITARIAN AVOWAL
A "FOUL CRIME"
UNDER COMMON LAW

Before, during, and long after Thomas Jefferson's time, the common law of England, followed in America, made it a crime to deny, with or without argument, any assumption or doctrine peculiar to orthodox Christianity. The prosecution of Daniel Isaac Eaton, in England in 1812, exemplifies the law and the temper of informers, prosecutors, and judges. The prosecutor in Eaton's case declaimed:

> He denies the miracles, the divinity, the resurrection, and the ascension of our Saviour; he contradicts His existence as the Son of God. . . . Ought not he who wishes to remove from society that which best unites it together be called on to answer for SO FOUL A CRIME?[1]

Prosecutors and judges imputed evil "wishes" to the denyers, and "ill tendency" to unbelieving speech. Treating Eaton's denials as "doctrines," the prosecutor said, with fervor:

> The effect of such doctrines on society at large, on every individual who composes a part of it—the evil consequences which must inevitably be produced by them, if they were generally disseminated, and took root in the minds of those by whom they were perused, would be dreadful in the extreme! . . . We are now proceeding against the defendant . . . for an offense as serious to the well-being of society as any that can be imagined. . . .

Eaton's denials were of doctrines which Jefferson later characterized as artificial systems.[2] Eaton had published Paine's

Examination of the Passages . . . Called Prophecies concerning Jesus Christ. It argued, among other things, that the prophecy in Isaiah 7:4 was not as represented in Matthew 1:23. Of the essay as a whole, Lord Ellenborough, the judge, told the jury: "I leave it to you as twelve Christian men to decide whether this is not a most blasphemous libel."

The common law in Jefferson's time and later was so understood and applied as to make Eaton's judge declare to the jury that "to *deny* the truths of the book which is the foundation of our faith *has never been permitted.*" He did not concede that some verses in the "book" may not be "truths."[3]

Jefferson, possibly remotely, is connected with the Eaton case because of the fact that Eaton obtained Paine's writings from Jefferson's friend William Duane (1750-1835), editor of *Aurora* at Philadelphia.[4]

Eaton in his defense argued as scholarly as was possible at that time in opposition to the doctrine of the Trinity, citing early authors, such as Cerinthus, who maintained that Jesus could not have been born of a virgin. He quoted Tillemont on the Ebionites. One passage in Eaton's paper was:

> . . . those witnesses who declare against the creeds and belief of the present day . . . were either contemporary with the apostles, as the Gnostics, the Essenians, the Ebionites, and Cerinthians, or had their history of Jesus Christ from those who had been perfectly instructed . . . (St. Clement of Alexandria, book VII, 761). . . .

But the judge, Lord Ellenborough, then told the jury:

> That paper, from the beginning to the end, was the most opprobrious invective against what we have been always accustomed to regard as holy and sacred—the religion of our country.

Undoubtedly Eaton had consulted the same ancient writings which Joseph Priestley studied before writing the two books, of which Jefferson wrote to Adams on August 22, 1813:

> I have read his [Priestley's] *Corruptions of Christianity* & *Early Opinions of Jesus, over and over again.* . . . These writings have never been answered, nor can be answered, by quoting historical proofs, as they have done, for these facts therefore I cling to their learning, so much superior to my own.

Eaton explained how his grandfather prevented him from becoming a Catholic. Continuing, he said:

> I therefore made it my study to examine the Bible with their [Catholics'] accounts of the saints; in doing which, I found the Bible so full of contradictions, and so full of wonderful things, that it induced me to examine this said Bible itself.

Thereupon Lord Ellenborough, the judge, interrupted, and said:

> Defendant, I must inform you that this is not to be made use of as an opportunity for you to revile the Christian religion; and if you persist in aspersing it, I will not only silence you, but I will animadvert on your conduct as an offence of the grossest kind against the dignity of the court. . . . I will not suffer the Christian religion to be reviled, while I sit in this court, and possess the power of preventing it.

In the course of his argument, Eaton said:

> For I cannot, nor ever could, perceive any, the smallest similarity, between the God of the Jews and the God of the Christians, as supposed to be worshipped in the present day.

The judge interrupted thus:

> You must see that this is unfit for yourself to read, or for us to hear. If you go on in this manner, I must order your address to be handed to the officer, and he, when reading it, must pause, and omit every offensive sentence. I tell you once more, that I will not permit the Christian religion to be reviled. . . .

The only answer the prosecutor made was this:

> My lord, I rise only to assert my right to reply: for I shall not give any importance to that which has fallen from the defendant, by making any observations on it.

Lord Ellenborough told the jury:

> In a free country, where religion is fenced round by the laws, and where that religion depends on the doctrines that are derived from the sacred writings, *to deny the truths* of the book which is the foundation of our faith *has never been permitted.* I am sure no impunity will be given to the offence by the verdict you will return today. I leave it to you as twelve Christian men to decide whether this is not a most blasphemous and impious libel.

The aged and infirm Eaton, being found "guilty," was sentenced to eighteen months' imprisonment and to stand in the pillory once a month, where he would undergo mental humiliation and physical torture. The prosecution and sentence impelled the poet Shelley to publish *Letter to Lord Ellenborough.* He there said:

> I hesitate not to affirm that the opinions which Mr. Eaton sustained, when undergoing that mockery of a trial, at which your lordship presided, appear to me more true and good than

those of his accuser, but were they false as the visions of a Calvinist, it still would be the duty of those who love liberty and virtue to raise their voice indignantly against a reviving system of persecution—against the coercively repressing any opinion, which, if false, needs but the opposition of truth; which, if true, in spite of force must ultimately prevail.

Unbelievers unknown to fame were prosecuted under the common law. The prominent, like Anthony Collins, were at first harassed only by "answers." Deistic writings of the seventeenth century, by authors too eminent to be imprisoned and sent to the pillory, led to the enactment of the statute of 9 William III, c. 32 (1698), which imposed disability to hold public office, and other penalties, on apostate Christians who "deny any one of the persons in the Holy Trinity to be God . . . or the Holy Scriptures . . . to be of divine authority." Thereafter the eminent writers so wrote as to avoid expressly making any of the criminal denials. Gibbon used this language:

> Under the reign of Tiberius, the whole earth, or at least a celebrated province of the Roman empire, was involved in a preternatural darkness of three hours. Even this miraculous event, which ought to have excited the wonder, curiosity, and the devotion of mankind, passed without notice in an age of science and history.

Soon after Shelley's denunciation of the Eaton prosecution, Parliament repealed the Holy Trinity clause, and so ostensibly emancipated Unitarian preachers. But laymen denying *any* part of the Holy Scriptures continued to be liable to all the penalties imposed on Eaton. Also a gift for Unitarianism remained unlawful,[5] as was a bequest for "the spread of Secular principles."[6] Unitarian property rights were not protected until the Dissenters' Chapels Act of 1844.[7]

All the prosecutions for "blasphemy" brought under the

common law, as distinguished from statutory law, conformed to an opinion written December 17, 1796, by John Bayley when advising a society complaining of Thomas Paine's *Age of Reason* after Part II thereof in 1795 "excited a general avidity to read the book, particularly among the middling and lower classes of life."[8] Bayley wrote:

> There can be no doubt that the pamphlet alluded to may be prosecuted at common law as a libel on the religion of the state. It was decided in Taylor's Case, I Ventris 293, and 3 Keble 607, that blasphemy was not only an offence to God and religion, but a crime against the laws, state, and government; and therefore, punishable by indictment: for to say religion is a cheat, is to dissolve all those obligations whereby civil societies are preserved; and to reproach the Christian religion is to speak in subversion of the law; and the defendant was sentenced to stand three times in the pillory, to pay a fine of one thousand marks and to find sureties for his good behaviour for life. . . . But the case of King against Woolston, Fitzgibbon 64, and Strange 834, is decisive.[9]

The common law crime of blasphemy, under which Eaton was prosecuted, was a judgemade invention "in Taylor's case" in 1676, after Atwood's Case in 1617, where offending words were treated as a disturbance of the peace which could be punished by temporal courts. In 1703 came the prosecution of Thomas Emlyn (1663-1741), "the first preacher to describe himself as a unitarian."[10] All he had done was to write a book in self-defense.[11] During the reigns of Mary, Elizabeth, and James I, there were executions of anti-Trinitarians under heresy laws.

The common law of blasphemy, as invented in Taylor's case, and applied in Woolston's Case in 1729, was revived in 1796 against a seller of Paine's *Age of Reason* in England, but no prosecution occurred in America after Benjamin Franklin's grandson Franklin Bache became consignee of

15,000 copies. A deluge of clerical pamphlets did follow, one entitled *An Investigation of that False, Fabulous and Blasphemous Misrepresentation of Truth, set forth by Thomas Paine, in his two volumes, entitled The Age of Reason, etc.*[12]

Eaton's case reminds of the popular expression "union of Church and State," which implies joint benevolence, but the judicial and ecclesiastical cruelty exhibited suggests that there was an alliance between tyrannical religion and subservient law, of which Shakespeare was thinking when in *The Merchant of Venice* he made Bassanio say:

> The world is still deceived by ornament,
> In law, what plea so tainted and corrupt,
> But, being seasoned with a gracious voice,
> Obscures the show of evil? In religion,
> What damned error, but some sober brow
> Will bless it and approve it with a text,
> Hiding its grossness with fair ornament.

That appears consistent with Jefferson's observation that "the alliance between Church and State in England has ever made their judges accomplices in the frauds of the clergy."[13]

Chapter Three

"BLASPHEMY" AND WITCHCRAFT STATUTES

Blackstone wrote in *Commentaries* (1770):

> Our forefathers were strong believers when they enacted, by statute of 33 Hen. VIII., c. 8, all witchcraft and sorcery to be felony without benefit of clergy; and again, by statute 1 Jac. I., c. 12, that all persons invoking any evil spirit, . . . should be guilty of felony without benefit of clergy, and suffer death.

Those statutes were repealed in 1736. "Benefit of clergy" meant a practice ordinarily used to exempt clergymen from a death penalty. To prevent its use in America, Congress prohibited it on April 30, 1790.[1]

When in 1665 Lord Hale ordered the hanging of Rose Cullender and Amy Duny as "witches," he opined "that there were such creatures as witches . . . first, the Scriptures had affirmed so much."[2] Robert Sherringham was a prosecuting witness, and this was a part of his testimony: " . . . so soon as his sows pigged, the pig would leap and caper, and immediately fall down and die."

The hanging of nineteen persons, and pressing one to death, in 1692 at Salem, Massachusetts, was "in accordance with English law."[3] The *Body of Liberties*, a code prepared by Nathaniel Ward (1578-1652), contained this clause:

> If any man or woman be a witch (that is hath or consulteth with a familiar spirit) they shall be put to death [Ex. 22:18; Lev. 20:27; Deut. 18:10].

Following Deuteronomy 18:10, cited in code, are the words

"or a consulter with a familiar spirit." In 1641 the witchcraft statute of James I (1603) was still in effect.

The *Body of Liberties* was mainly a blasphemy statute, and provided:

> If any person shall blaspheme the name of God, the Father, Sonne or Holy Ghost, with direct, express, presumptious or high handed blasphemie, or shall curse God in the like manner, he shall be put to death. Lev. 24:15,16.

Notwithstanding that "blasphemy" became, after 1617, a crime under the judge-made common law, statutes were enacted in several colonies. John Adams, noticing that the statute of *his* state, Massachusetts, named every book of the King James version, and made "cursing or reproaching the Holy Word of God" a crime, wrote to Jefferson on January 23, 1825: "Books that cannot bear examination, certainly ought not to be established as divine inspiration by penal laws."[4]

The Act of 1697, though not that of 1782, designated one of the penalties as "boring through the tongue with a red-hot iron." Both acts "established," by making it a crime to deny, the doctrine of "final judging of the world."

What the Massachusetts Legislature meant by "final judging of the world" in the Statute of 1782 is determinable from Chapter XXXII of the Westminster Confession of 1648, particularly the words: ". . . At the last day. . . . And all the dead shall be raised up with the selfsame bodies, and none other, . . . which shall be united again to their souls for ever. The bodies of the unjust shall by the power of Christ raised to dishonour. . . ." The statute with respect to "final judging" may still be found in the Massachusetts General Laws of 1921 (Sec. 36, Ch. 272). It begins thus:

> That if any person shall wilfully blaspheme the holy name of God, by *denying*, cursing, or contumeliously reproaching God,

His creation, government, or *final judging of the world.* . . .

In 1662 Michael Wigglesworth wrote the "Last Judgment," the poem containing the lines:

> For day and night, in their despite,
>   Their torment's smoke ascendeth,
> Their pain and grief have no relief;
>   Their anguish never endeth.
> There must they lie and never die,
>   Though dying every day;
> There must they dying ever lie,
>   And not consume away.

The *Body of Liberties* also established Jehovah as the colony's God. The enacting clause was:

> If any man . . . shall have or worship any other God, but the Lord God, he shall be put to death [Deut. 13:6, 10; Deut. 17:2, 6; Ex. 22:20].

The biblical texts cited, and adopted as part of the law, are replete with the phrase "Jehovah *thy* God." The "Lord God" of Genesis 24:27, as printed in 1641, was "Jehovah, the God" of Genesis 24:27, as it reads in the revision of 1901.

The John Adams letter on the Massachusetts Statute of 1782 was as follows:

> We think ourselves possessed, or, at least we boast that we are so, of liberty of conscience on all subjects, and of the right of free inquiry and private judgment in all cases, and yet how far are we from those exalted privileges in fact: There exists, I believe, through out the whole Christian world, a law which makes it blasphemy to deny or doubt the divine inspiration of all the books of the Old and New Testaments, from Genesis to Revelation. In most countries of Europe it is punished by fire at the stake, or the rack, or the wheel. In England itself

it is punished by boring through the tongue with a red-hot poker. In America it is not much better; even in our own Massachusetts, which I believe, upon the whole, is as temperate and moderate in religious zeal as most of the States, a law was made in the latter end of the last century, repealing the cruel punishments of the former laws, but substituting fine and imprisonment upon all those blasphemers upon any book of the Old Testament or New. Now, what free inquiry, when a writer must surely encounter the risk of fine or imprisonment for adducing any argument for investigation into the divine authority of those books? Who would run the risk of translating Volney's *Recherches?* Who would run the risk of translating Dupuis? But I cannot enlarge upon this subject, though I have it much at heart. I think such laws a great embarrassment, great obstructions to the improvement of the human mind. Books that cannot bear examination, certainly ought not to be established as divine inspiration by penal laws. It is true, few persons appear desirous to put such laws in execution, and it is also true that some few persons are hardy enough to venture to depart from them. But as long as they continue in force as laws, the human mind must make an awkward and clumsy progress in its investigations. I wish they were repealed. The substance and essence of Christianity, as I understand it, is eternal and unchangeable, and will bear examination forever, but it has been mixed with extraneous ingredients, which I think will not bear examination, and they ought to be separated.

The Massachusetts Statute of 1697 named for protection each of the "books of the Old and New Testaments," as found in the King James version. In 1833, under statute then in effect, Abner Kneeland was convicted for publishing, without argument, an avowal of nonbelief "in the God of the Universalists." As to when, if ever, such avowal was lawful, the court said:

... the simple and sincere avowal of disbelief in the existence and attributes of a supreme, intelligent being, upon suitable and proper occasions . . . as where a man is called as a witness . . . and questioned upon his belief, he is not only permitted, but bound, by every consideration of moral honesty, to avow his unbelief, if it exist . . . he may avow it confidentially to a friend, in the hope of gaining new light on the subject, even perhaps whilst he regrets his unbelief.[5]

At the trial, the defendant's counsel read Jefferson's letter to Major Cartwright. Jefferson's name was on the masthead of Kneeland's *The Boston Investigator*, for which Frances Wright (1795-1852), favorably known to Jefferson and Lafayette, once worked.[6]

In February, 1926, the statute was invoked against Anthony Bimba at Brockton, Massachusetts. Acquittal resulted.[7]

Prosecutions under statute have taken place in Delaware, Connecticut, Maine, and New Jersey.[8] New Jersey judges have recently flaunted the survival of their statute,[9] which has since 1821 prescribed fine and imprisonment. In 1642 it fixed a death penalty, and in 1784 this was changed to whipping on the naked body.

The Maryland "Toleration" Act of 1649 included a "confiscation" clause in the following passage:

> . . . whatsoever persons . . . shall deny our Saviour to be the Son of God, or shall deny the Holy Trinity . . . of the Godhead of any of the said Three Persons of the Trinity . . . shall be punished with death, and *confiscation* . . . of all his or her land and goods to the lord proprietor and his heirs.[10]

What would happen to Unitarians, or to such Christians who believed according to Matthew I:16 as written in the Sinaitic Palimpsest: "Joseph begat Jesus, who is called the Christ."?[11]

There was no "toleration" of anyone who would say, as Jefferson later did in a letter to John Adams on April 11, 1823:

. . . and the day will come, when the mystical generation of Jesus, by the Supreme Being as His Father, in the womb of a virgin, will be classed with the fable of the generation of Minerva in the brain of Jupiter.[12]

In 1723 the Lord Proprietor and Assembly of Maryland enacted a statute on Blasphemy which provided that the person "convicted by verdict or confession, shall for the first offense be bored through the tongue and fined 20 pounds sterling . . . and that for the second offense, the offender . . . shall be stigmatized by burning on the forehead with the letter B, and fined forty pounds . . . and that for the third offense, the offender . . . shall suffer death without benefit of clergy."

If the Maryland Statute had not been repealed, it would have been also the law in the District of Columbia, the Act of Congress of February 27, 1801, providing that the "laws of the state of Maryland . . . shall be and continue in force . . . in the District of Columbia."[13]

In Virginia, Dale's Code, in effect 1610-19, made impious speech of the Trinity "punishable by death." After 1676 all the colonies had the judge-made common law on "blasphemy." In 1705 the legislature of Virginia passed, or adopted, a statute in the words of the English Act of 1698, cited in the books as Act 9 William III., c. 32. It did not affect the common law, which remained in force and was applied against lowly and obscure offenders. The Act of 1698 was aimed at influential persons "having been educated in, or at any time having made any profession of, the Christian religion." In 1698 deistic literature had accumulated—for example, works of Charles Blount—which provoked Parliament to declare in the Preamble:

Whereas many persons have of late years openly avowed and published many blasphemous and impious opinions contrary to the doctrine and principles of the Christian religion, greatly tending to the dishonour of Almighty God, and may prove destructive to the peace and welfare of this kingdom: Wherefore, for the more effectual suppressing of the said detestable crimes, be it enacted by the King's most excellent Majesty, by and with the advice and consent of the Lords spiritual and temporal, and the Commons in this present Parliament assembled, and by the authority of the same, that. . . .

Then followed a provision that if any "person or persons" above described shall "deny any one of the persons in the Holy Trinity to be God," or "shall deny" the doctrines specified, for a first offense there would be a disability to hold office, and other disabilities would be imposed for a second offense. The result of the English Act of 1698 was that thereafter deistic authors guarded their language well, to avoid the criminal denials, as may appear from the subsequent works of Gibbon, Hume, and Middleton, the latter being one of Jefferson's favorite authors.

Before the American Revolution the English statute was in effect in the colonies also, and that caused Jefferson in 1776 to introduce in the House of Delegates the resolution:

. . . that all and every act or statute of Great Britain . . . which renders criminal the maintaining of any opinion in matters of religion . . . or which prescribes punishments for the same, ought to be declared henceforth as of no validity or force within this commonwealth.[14]

A Virginia statute, accordant with that resolution, was then passed, and in 1781 Jefferson had occasion to write, in *Notes on Virginia:*

Statutory oppressions in religion being thus wiped away (by act of 1776), we remain at present under those only imposed by the common law, or by our own acts of assembly. . . .

The judge-made "common law" on "blasphemy" arose in 1617 by a decision that temporal courts may act because offensive words on religion have a tendency to disturb the peace.[15] In 1676 Lord Hale devised the slogan: "Christianity is parcel of the laws of England."[16]

In a Connecticut colony a code of 1650 on witchcraft and blasphemy was practically the same as that of *Body of Liberties*, and it added a death penalty for burglary committed "on the Lord's day." A Pennsylvania statute was invoked against an accused in 1824, and Colonel Robert G. Ingersoll was threatened with it in 1884.[17]

In England, there was also a blasphemy act of 1650 so worded as to apply to the preachings by Quakers.[18]

When Parliament decided to punish one of its own members for "blasphemy," it proceeded on its usurped power only. In 1650, John Fry, a member, published an answer to some accusation made against him by another member. The Parliament's "Committee on Plundered Ministers" thereupon accused Fry of having denied the Trinity, calling it "a chaffy and absurd Opinion of Three Persons, or Subsistences, in the Godhead." The Committee quoted from still another Fry book, and reported: "That both said books, throughout, are against . . . Doctrine and assertions of the true religion." Parliament ordered the books burned and Fry "disabled to sit as a member of this House" of Parliament.[19]

John Asgill (1659-1738) was expelled by both the Parliament of Ireland and that of England for having published a "blasphemous" pamphlet in 1700. This was of interest to Jefferson, since he acquired a copy of "Mr. Asgill's defense upon his expulsion from the House of Commons of Great Britain in 1707."[20] Both Parliaments ordered the burning of Asgill's book, on the assumption that it "contained many profane and blasphemous expressions highly reflecting upon the Christian Religion."[21]

Chapter Four

THE WRIT
DE HAERETICO COMBURENDO

The burning of heretics by mobs was once sanctioned by custom.[1] Frederick II (1194-1250) became Emperor of Rome in 1220. In 1224 he issued edicts that obstinate heretics be burned and penitent ones imprisoned.[2]

In 1378 Gregory XI urged the English bishops to burn "Lollards" (followers of John Wycliffe). First they forged an act purporting to give them power to arrest and imprison. Next, in 1400, Arundel sponsored the Act of Henry IV, which enabled the *diocean* alone to sentence for heresy, and have the sheriff burn the accused, "to strike fear into the minds of others. . . ."[3] The writ *de haeretico comburendo* for the burning of William Sawtre was issued, and he burned, March 2, 1400. The statute was not finally passed until eight days later.[4]

William Stubbs (1815-1901), English bishop and historian, in *Constitutional History of England* states that an Albigensian was burned in London in 1210. The historian also shows that during and after 1414 the laws were still further extended by leaving heresy undefined and permitting the "ordinary," an ecclesiastic having original jurisdiction in ecclesiastical causes, to deliver over to the sheriff to be burned any person whom *he* found guilty of heresy. Thirty-eight persons were burned in 1414. Dr. Stubbs writes of cases in 1417, 1422, 1430, 1431, 1438, 1440, 1466, and 1467. Later dates and cases are mentioned in Stephen's *History of the Criminal Law of England*.

Stephen quotes Arundel's question to William Sawtre, in 1400, as follows:

. . . whether that material bread, being round and white, prepared and disposed for the sacrament of the body of Christ upon the altar, wanting nothing that is meet and requisite thereunto, by virtue of the sacramental words being by the priest rightly pronounced, be altered and changed into the very body of Christ, and ceaseth any more to be material and very bread or not.

In 1539 came the Act of the Six Articles (31 Henry VIII, c. 14) enforcing conformity to six of the strongest points in the Roman Catholic religion, and providing "that every one who denied the doctrine of transubstantiation, or depraved the sacrament, should be burnt as a heretic."[5] Prior to the Act of the Six Articles, the ordinary could, and did in 1533, bring about the burning of John Frith (1503-33) for denying that the doctrines of purgatory and of transubstantiation were necessary articles of faith.

After the accession of Elizabeth I (November 17, 1558) heresy was redefined, and acts enforced by Queen Mary were abolished. According to Jefferson's brief notes, an act of the first year of Elizabeth provided that "the diocean may burn" and that there were "Arians burnt" in the seventeenth year (1575).[6] Of burnings in that year, John M. Robertson wrote:

When in 1575 the law *De haeretico comburendo*, which had slept for seventeen years, was set to work anew under Elizabeth, the first victims were Dutch Anabaptists. Of a congregation of them at Aldgate, twenty-seven were imprisoned, of whom ten were burned, and the rest deported. Two others, John Wielmacker and Hendrich Ter Woort, were anti-Trinitarians, and were burned accordingly. Foxe appealed to the Queen to appoint any punishment short of death, or even that of hanging, rather than the horrible death by burning; but in vain. "All parties at the time concurred" in approving the course taken. Orthodoxy was rampant.[7]

Matthew Hamond was burned in 1579 for declaring the

New Testament "a fable, Christ a mere sinful man, erected into an abominable idol, the Holy Ghost a nonentity, and the sacraments useless." In 1587 Peter Cole, and in 1589 Francis Kett, were burned. Christopher Marlowe (1564-93) would have been executed if he had not been privately killed. Biographies of the above-named men are given in the *Dictionary of National Biography*.

Legate was burned at Smithfield, March 18, 1612. In 1655 Thomas Fuller (1608-61) listed thirteen "wicked errors" of Legate, one being: "Christ was not God from everlasting, but began to be God when he took flesh of the Virgin Mary."[8] This contradicted the following in the Anglican creed: "The Son, which is the Word of the Father, begotten *from everlasting* of the Father. . . ." Fuller prefaced his list in this manner:

> Before we set down his pestilent opinions; may the writer and reader fence themselves with prayer to God, against the infection thereof: lest otherwise, touching such pitch (though with but the bare mention) defile us, casually tempting a temptation in us, and awaken some corruption which otherwise would sleep silently in our souls.

Edward Wightman, a "Baptist,"[9] was burned in April, 1612. The historian Fuller says:

> Mary Magdelene was once possessed with seven devils, but ten several heresies were laid to Wightman's charge, namely, those of Ebion, Corinthus, Valentinian, Arius, Macedonius, Simon Magnus, Manes, Manichaeus, Photinus, and of the Anabaptists. Lord! What are we when God leaves us? [10]

Jefferson's note on Arians was:

> . . . X^n [Christian] heretics. They avow there was a time when the Son was not, that he was created in time mutable in

nature, & like the angels liable to sin; they deny the three persons in the trinity to be of the same essence. Erasmus and Grotius were Arians.[11]

Erasmus found that the verse in I John 5:7 as then printed, regarding the "three witnesses," was an interpolation.[12] Jefferson thought the interpolation crafty.[13]

In October, 1666, an attempt was made to revive the writ *de haeretico comburendo* against Thomas Hobbes (1588-1679) for his authorship of *Leviathan*. A biographical sketch of Hobbes includes the following:

> . . . but it was not till 1666 that he felt himself seriously in danger. In that year the Great Fire of London, following on the Great Plague, roused the superstitious fears of the people, and the House of Commons embodied the general feeling in a bill against atheism and profaneness. On the 17th of October it was ordered that the committee to which the bill was referred "should be empowered to receive information touching such books as tend to atheism, blasphemy and profaneness, or against the essence and attributes of God, and in particular the book published in the name of one White, and the book of Mr. Hobbes called the *Leviathan,* and to report the matter with their opinion to the House." [14]

The *Leviathan* is still occasionally republished, and was appreciatively read by the late Mr. Justice Oliver Wendell Holmes.[15]

The writ in question was not used after Wightman's case. Instead, prosecutions were by indictment, and there was no death penalty.

In 1781, and before the Statute of 1786 was enacted, Jefferson referred to the writ in this passage in *Notes on Virginia:*

> Statutory oppressions in religion being thus wiped away (by act of 1776), we remain at present under those only imposed by the common law, or by our own acts of assembly. At com-

mon law, *heresy* was a capital offense, punishable by burning.
Its definition was left to the ecclesiastical judges, before whom
the conviction was, till the statute of 1 El. c. 1 circumscribed
it, by declaring, that nothing should be deemed heresy, but
what had been so determined by authority of the canonical
scriptures, or by one of the first four general councils, or by
other council, having for the grounds of their declaration the
express and plain words of the scriptures. . . . The execution
is by the writ *De haeretico comburendo.* . . .

The writ itself was not at common law. Mr. Justice Morton
of the Supreme Judicial Court of Massachusetts had occasion
to say:

It has been supposed that heresy was a crime at common
law, and the existence of the writ *de haeretico comburendo,*
in the Register, is considered as proof of it. But Lord Commissioner Whitelocke, in his sensible though quaint argument
in Nayler's case, 5 Howell's *State Trials,* 825, refutes this
notion. He says this writ was not contained in the ancient
manuscript register, but was of later date and brought in by
Archbishop Arundel, in Henry the 4th's time, for the punishment and suppression of the Lollards.[16]

Chapter Five

HISTORIC EXAMPLES OF
"TYRANNY OVER THE MIND"

EXPLOITATION OF POVERTY, IGNORANCE, AND CREDULITY

In 1814 Jefferson said of the poverty in England:

> . . . what does it [England] defend? The pauperism of the
> lowest class, the abject oppression of the laboring, and the
> luxury, the riot, the domination and the vicious happiness of
> the aristocracy. In their hands, the paupers are used as tools
> to maintain their own wretchedness, and to keep down the
> laboring portion by shooting them whenever the desperation
> produced by the cravings of their stomachs drives them into
> riots.[1]

The riots and distress of the Luddites at an earlier time
were not forgotten.[2] Jefferson noticed how both church and
state exploited the people, once writing:

> Government, as well as religion, has furnished its schisms, its
> persecutions, and its devices for fattening idleness on the earn-
> ings of the people. It has its hierarchy of emperors, kings,
> princes, and nobles, as that has of popes, cardinals, archbishops,
> bishops and priests. In short, cannibals are not to be found in
> the wilds of America only, but are reveling on the blood of
> every living people.[3]

In 1823 Jefferson remembered, or observed, that:

> The doctrines of Europe were, that men in numerous asso-
> ciations cannot be restrained within the limits of order and
> justice, but by forces physical and moral, wielded over them
> by authorities independent of their will. Hence their organiza-

42

tion of kings, hereditary nobles, and priests. Still further to
constrain the brute force of the people, they deem it necessary
to keep them down by hard labor, poverty and ignorance,
and to take from them, as from bees, so much of their earnings, as that unremitting labor shall be necessary to obtain
a sufficient surplus barely to sustain a scanty and miserable
life. And these earnings they apply to maintain their privileged
orders in splendor and idleness, to fascinate the eyes of the
people, and excite in them an humble adoration and submis-
sion, as to an order of superior beings.[4]

For such doctrines, Jefferson would substitute:

> ... that man was a rational animal, endowed by nature with
> rights, and with an innate sense of justice; and that he could
> be restrained from wrong and protected in right, by moderate
> powers, confided to persons of his own choice. . . .[5]

Jefferson agreed with John Adams that the "fifty-two
volumes in folio of *Acta Sanctorum*" contain "the most enormous mass of lies, frauds, hypocrisy, and imposture, that ever
was heaped together on this globe."[6] From *Acta*, Adams
could have learned that, as he wrote, "miracles after miracles
have rolled down in torrents, wave succeeding wave in the
Catholic church. . . ."[7] Jefferson's calling the Presbyterian
clergy "Aruspices of Modern Paganism"[8] could have resulted
from reading Cicero's *De Divinatione*, which mentioned that
Cato "could not understand how one haruspex could keep
from bursting into laughter whenever he met one of the
brethren."[9] Of contemporary "hierophants" Jefferson observed that they have "privileged days . . . of moulding . . .
minds as wax in the hollow of their hands."[10]

Of course the "hierophants" used biblical texts as literally
true in *every* instance, and Jefferson was prompted to advise
Peter Carr: "Read the Bible . . . as you would Livy or Tacitus."[11] When Carr thereafter read the "spittle" verse in John

9:6, he might have noticed that Hume read his Tacitus, and he wrote: "One of the best attested miracles in all profane history, is that which Tacitus reports of Vespasian, who cured a blind man in Alexandria by means of his spittle."

Another of Jefferson's observations on the "priesthood" is the following:

> The mild and simple principles of the Christian philosophy would produce too much calm, too much regularity of good, to extract from its disciples a support for a numerous priesthood, were they not to sophisticate it, ramify it, split it into hairs, and twist its texts till they cover the divine morality of its author with mysteries, and require a priesthood to explain them. The Quakers seem to have discovered this. They have no priests, therefore no schisms. They judge of the text by the dictates of common sense and common morality.[12]

John Adams had occasion to use the following language:

> . . . the question before mankind is . . . whether offices, spiritual and temporal, are instituted by men, or whether they are self-created and institute themselves. Whether they were or were not brought down from heaven in a phial of holy oil, sent by the Holy Ghost, by an angel incarnated in a dove, to anoint the head of Clovis, a more cruel tyrant than Frederick or Napoleon.[13]

Clovis was the "most Christian king," according to Pope Anastasius.[14] "The story of the phial of holy oil brought from heaven by a white dove for the baptism of Clovis was *invented* by Archbishop Hincmar of Reims three centuries after the event."[15] Clovis was baptized in 496 and Hincmar lived 805-82. The "dove" story may have been inspired by familiarity with the Biblical text having the words "he saw the Spirit of God descending as a dove" (Matt. 3:16) and like expressions in Mark 1:10 and Luke 3:22. Such texts are still "gospel," and in 1921 the Supreme Court of Maine was horrified by Mockus's ridicule of the "dove" verses, and ardently upheld his conviction of "blasphemy."[16]

Jefferson's Preamble to his Statute for Religious Freedom shows he intended to remove the "temporal   punishments, or burthens" and "civil incapacitations" which had been inflicted on heterodox individuals. John Adams came to notice also the "lies," and on December 3, 1813, in a letter to Jefferson he quoted Juan Luis Vives (1497–1540): "There have been men who have thought it a great piece of piety, to invent lies for the sake of religion."[17] In 1668 Daniel Papenbrock (1628-1714) rejected some ecclesiastical stories "as fables."[18] John Adams said in a letter to Jefferson in February, 1814:

> E. G. Papebrock doubted . . . whether the face of Jesus Christ was painted on the handkerchief of St. Veronique, and whether the prepuce of the Saviour of the world, which was shown in the church of Antwerp, could be proved to be genuine? For these bold skepticisms he was libelled in pamphlets, and denounced by the Pope, and the Inquisition in Spain.[19]

Jefferson, too, was a target for lies. The third (1805) edition of Thomas Green Fessenden's *Democracy Unveiled* had this:

> We have it from good authority that Mr. Jefferson actually became initiated, while in Paris, into the mysteries of Illuminism, and his writings and conduct, since his embassy to France, display "internal evidence" of his being infected with the poison of *illuminated* principles.

The innuendo against Illuminism was itself false.[20] So also was an article in the *Palladium*, as to Jefferson and the "Goddess of Reason."[21]

Long before the campaign of 1800, August 6, 1798, the

Connecticut Courant published a statement which included: "[Jefferson] is the real Jacobin, the very child of Illumination, the foe of man, and the enemy of his country."[22] The allegation followed, and must have been provoked by a May 9, 1798, sermon of the Reverend Jedidiah Morse, which conformed to John Robison's book entitled *Proofs of a Conspiracy*, etc., published in 1797 in Edinburgh. The book alarmed the Reverend J. W. Snyder; and on August 22, 1798, he wrote to George Washington:

> A thought suggested itself to me that some of the [Masonic] Lodges in the United States might have caught the infection, and might cooperate with the Illuminati, or the Jacobin Clubs in France.[23]

After Robison's book, soon came one by Abbé Augustin Barruel, in England. It was Barruel's book that came to Jefferson's notice in 1799, and prompted him to write of it to Bishop Madison, January 31, 1800, stating that it (Barruel's book):

> . . . is the color for the ravings against him [Dr. Adam Weishaupt, founder of the Bavarian Illuminati] of Robinson, Barruel & Morse, whose real fears that the craft would be endangered by the spreading of information, reason, & natural morality among men. . . .[24]

The term "craft" was Jefferson's reference to the clerical profession.[25]

Alluding to the same "craft," Jefferson had occasion to say:

> You judge truly that I am not afraid of the priests. They have tried upon me all their various batteries, of pious whining, hypocritical canting, lying and slandering, without being able to give me one moment of pain.[26]

Notwithstanding it had available to it the writings of university scholars and Masonic writers, hereinbefore cited, the House Un-American Activities Committee in its 1931 Report No. 2290 followed the "Robison, Barruel & Morse" line, as Jefferson would call it, by adding an article by Congressman John E. Nelson, wherein the latter accused Dr. Adam Weishaupt of having "organized the order of the Illuminati, dedicated to the destruction of Christianity and all existing governments," and that the Communist Manifesto of 1848 was based on the "abolitions" alleged to have been advocated by Weishaupt.

CRUELTIES OF PRELATES AND PRIESTS

What Jefferson had in mind when drafting the clause of the Statute which provided "that no man shall . . . suffer on account of his religious opinions or belief" was later expressed in *Notes on Virginia*. One passage therein is:

> Millions of men, women and children, since the introduction of Christianity, have been burned, tortured, fined, imprisoned. . . .

The victims were called "heretics," and to physical suffering was, in many cases, added confiscation of the heretic's property, thus depriving children or heirs of any inheritance.

John Foxe (1516-87) in 1563 published his *Book of Martyrs*, dealing with persecutions by "Romish Prelates" in England and Scotland. In America, in 1843, the Presbyterian Board of Publications of Philadelphia published *The English Martyrology*, abridged from Foxe, by Charlotte Elizabeth, and therein the cruelties of prelates and allied secular officials are vividly set forth. Jefferson never mentioned "Romish Prelates" but thought of "the fire and faggots of Calvin and his victim Servetus."

Having acquired both of the books written by Lucilio

Vanini (1585-1619), Jefferson presumably learned from other sources that, for some words on nature as a power, Vanini was convicted as for "atheism," and that of his execution a Christian historian wrote:

> Before putting fire to the stake, Vanini was ordered to put forth his sacrilegious tongue for the knife. . . . It was necessary to employ pincers to draw it forth, and when the executioner's instrument . . . cut it off never was heard a more horrible cry. One might have thought he heard the bellowing of an ox which was being slaughtered.[27]

Being familiar with Scotch and English history, Jefferson presumably knew of the execution of Thomas Aikenhead, of whom Thomas Macaulay later wrote:

> . . . a student of eighteen, named Thomas Aikenhead, whose habits were studious and whose morals were irreproachable, had, in the course of his readings, met with some of the ordinary arguments against the Bible. . . . Trinity in unity, he said, was as much a contradiction as a square circle. . . .
> The ministers demanded not only the poor boy's death, but his speedy death, though it should be his eternal death. . . . Even from their pulpits they cried out for cutting him off. . . . The preachers, who were the boy's murderers, crowded round him at the gallows, and while he was struggling in the last agony, insulted heaven with prayers more blasphemous than anything that he had ever uttered. . . .[28]

The informer against Aikenhead was a "decoy who gave him the books and made him speak as he did."[29] "The spirit of the prosecution may be gathered from the facts that the boy broke down and pleaded penitence, and that the statute enacted the capital penalty only for obstinately persisting in the denial of any of the persons of the Trinity."[30] Scotland at that time, 1695, was still witch-hunting, and in 1708 burned a "witch" at Dornoch.[31]

The Jesuits of Bohemia destroyed all procurable copies of a history of the Thirty Years' War (1618-48) by John Amos Comenius (Komensky) in *Historia Persecutionum*. They inflicted upon non-Jesuits such sentences as this:

> The doctor Jessenius, rector of the Academy of Prague, while living shall have his tongue cut out, his body divided into quarters, his limbs hung at the cross roads; his head and his tongue shall be thrown into a sewer.[32]

In England, the first Article of the Act of the Six Articles (31 Henry VIII, c. 14) set forth the Catholic doctrine of transubstantiation. It was provided, a historian says:

> . . . that any one who should publish, preach, teach, say, affirm . . . or hold any opinion contrary to the first article, . . . together with their aiders, comforters, . . . should be deemed heretics, and suffer death by burning, without any abjuration, or benefit of the clergy or sanctuary, forfeiting also the whole of their property to the king, as in cases of high treason.[33]

The Statute is not overlooked in D. H. Montgomery's *The Leading Facts of English History* (2d ed., 1892).

Ann Askew (1517-46) as a Bible student came to disbelieve the doctrine of transubstantiation and was tried for heresy in 1545, but acquitted. In June, 1546, she was again accused, and convicted. She was put to the rack and her body stretched by the solicitor and by Lord Chancellor Wriothesley. Then she was left in prison for four weeks, and on July 16, 1546, she was burned at Smithfield in the presence of Wriothesley and other dignitaries. Wriothesley was made Earl of Southampton in 1547, as if being rewarded, which reminds of rewards later given to other heresy-hunters, and of Jefferson's Preamble to the Statute for Religious Freedom, where it says:

> . . . that it tends also to corrupt the principles of that very religion it is meant to encourage, by bribing, with a monopoly of worldly honours and emoluments, those who will externally profess and conform to it. . . .

Joan Boucher of Kent was burned in 1550 upon the insistent demand of Archbishop Cranmer, who needed no further rewards for conformity to contemporary orthodoxy as it was prior to Queen Mary.

In Massachusetts, October 18, 1659, Mary Dyer was sentenced to death as a Quaker disobeying banishment previously ordered because her opinion that she was "without sin" was one that "tends to overthrow the whole gospel," and her disobedience of banishment a breach of the biblical injunction to obey magistrates.[34]

Thomas Pooley was an industrious laborer who had never read or spoken anything of a freethinking nature; but in a moment of mental distraction he wrote upon a gate, according to the informer the Reverend Paul Bush, "Duloe stinks with the monster Christ's Bible." Pooley was prosecuted, without counsel, convicted, and sentenced to six months' imprisonment. A further imprisonment was added for his having said: "If they would burn their Bibles, and use the ashes for dressing the land, it would get rid of the potato disease." Mill in his essay *On Liberty* referred to that prosecution; and, when the historian Henry Thomas Buckle read that, he denounced the prosecution as "a revival of cruelty, a revival of bigotry, a revival of the tastes, habits, and feelings of those days of darkness which we might have hoped had gone forever."[35]

Some ministers of minority sects would be intolerant of brethren in an established church. On July 23, 1770 Jefferson wrote Peyton Randolph that James Ogilvie was seeking *episcopal* ordination, and "paid a visit to his father, a *Presbyterian* minister. . . . Yet, so wonderful is the dominion of bigotry over her votaries that on the first information of his purpose to receive episcopal ordination he shut him from his doors and abjured every parental duty."[36] Fifty years later Jefferson again noticed contemporary Presbyterian persecutive bigotry, and its power to make public opinion work as an accomplice.[37] The tyranny of that kind of "public opinion" is discussed in Chapter XII.

BAPTISTS AND THE PROSECUTION OF BENJAMIN KEACH

James Madison referred to persecution of Baptists in Virginia when he wrote:

> Poverty and luxury prevail among all sorts; pride, ignorance, and knavery among the priesthood, and vice and wickedness among the laity. This is bad enough, but it is not the worst I have to tell you. That diabolical, hell conceived principle of persecution rages among some; and to their eternal infamy, the clergy can furnish their quota of imps for such business. . . . There are at this time in the adjacent country not less than five or six well-meaning men in close jail for publishing their religious sentiments, which in the main are very orthodox.[38]

Being "very orthodox," the accused were not charged with either sedition or blasphemy but only with disturbing the peace.

Jefferson, having early acquired the four volumes of *State Trials*, published by Thomas Salmon in 1719, or a second edition with two more volumes edited by Sollum Emlyn in 1730, probably read the report of the trial of the Baptist Reverend Benjamin Keach in 1664. Keach was charged with publishing "damnable positions" in "one seditious and venomous book" entitled *Child's Instructor: or, A New and Easy Primer*.

One of the offending "positions" was in these words:

> Q.   What are the right subjects of baptism?
> A.   Believers, or Godly men and women only, who can make confessions of their faith and repentence.[39]

Sir Robert Hyde, the judge, told the jury: "This is contrary to the Book of Common Prayer, for that appoints infants to be baptized, as well as men and women."

Hyde's Book of Common Prayer was not inconsistent with the following declaration of the Catholic theologian Fulgentius:

> . . . not only men who have come to the use of reason, but infants dying, whether in their mother's womb or after birth, without baptism in the name of the Father, Son and Holy Ghost, are punished with everlasting punishment in eternal fire.[40]

On the *Child's Instructor's* answer to "How shall it then go with the saints?" the judge said:

> This is contrary to the Creed in the Book of Common-Prayer, and is an old heresy, which was cast out of the Church a thousand years ago, and was likewise condemned by the Council of Constance about 500 years ago, and hath lain dead ever since, till now this *rascal* hath revived it.

The judge, Sir Robert Hyde, was himself worse than a mere rascal, according to a speech by John Dunning (1731-83), Lord Ashburton, in the House of Commons, December 6, 1770.[41]

Keach was sentenced to imprisonment and the pillory. He was "carried to the pillory at Ailsbury; where he stood full two hours to a minute, was denied the liberty of speaking to the spectators, and had his hands as well as his head carefully kept in the pillory the whole time." Referring to the pillory, the judge had said: "And there your book shall be openly burnt before your face by the common hangman, in disgrace of you and your doctrine."

The Virginia Baptists suffered enough to favor legislative action. The Declaration of the Virginia Association of Baptists (December 25, 1776) recited that "it is contrary to the principles of Reason and Justice that any should be compelled to contribute to the Maintenance of a Church with which their Conscience will not permit them to join, and from which they can therefore receive no Benefit," and that this "is not merely the opinion of the Dissenters (whose hardships on that score have *feelingly convinced* them of the Truth of it . . .). . . ."

Jefferson's "wall of separation" letter to the Danbury Baptists had also the words "that the legislative powers of government reach actions only, and not opinions." Robert Hall (1764-1831), a Baptist, became in 1793 the author of *Apology for the Freedom of the Press*, a copy of which came to Jefferson's library. Baptists still think of John Leland as an associate of Jefferson, and as "the man who promoted the First Amendment."[42] On behalf of *all* denominations, Jefferson wrote:

> . . . it behooves every man who values liberty of conscience for himself to resist invasions of it in the case of others, or their case may, by change of circumstances, become his own.[43]

QUAKERS AND THE PROSECUTION OF JAMES NAYLER

In Massachusetts in 1659 three Quakers were sentenced to be hanged under a statute punishing for a second return after banishment. The opinion of the Court included this language:

> 3. . . . in this story of Solomon and Shimei, it is recorded (1 Kings 2) how Solomon confined Shimei to Jerusalem, charg-

ing him upon pain of death not to go out thence, and telling him, if he did he should die for it; which confinement when Shimei had broken, . . . Solomon would not spare him, but put him to death; and if execution of death be lawful for breach of confinement, may not the same be said for breach of *banishment?*[44]

(Virginia enacted a similar Quaker banishment statute in 1659.[45] In England Quakers were prosecuted as for blasphemy, and would be deemed guilty thereof if their religious views on sin were inconsistent with orthodox doctrines.)[46]

The Massachusetts prosecution was under statute for "breach of banishment," prescribing a death penalty, justified by the judges as follows:

> Now the commandment of God is plain, that he that presumes to speak lies in the name of the Lord, and turn people out of the way which the Lord hath commanded to walk in, such a one must not live, but be *put to death*. Zech. 13:3; Deut. 13:6; 18:2, and if the doctrines of the quakers be not such, let the wise judge.

Earlier in England James Nayler, a Quaker, was prosecuted as for "blasphemy" by the House of Commons, and the death penalty was avoided only because the members voted 96 to 82 against it. There was much appeal to Leviticus and Deuteronomy.[47] The penalties inflicted on Nayler included whippings, the pillory, and boring through the tongue with a red hot iron.[48]

In 1650-51 there were several imprisonments, including that of George Fox, under a Blasphemy Act of 1650, for charges to which Quakers were peculiarly liable because of their doctrine of perfection.[49]

A concise history of persecutions of Quakers is given in the 11th (1910) edition of *Encyclopaedia Britannica*, Volume

11, page 224. In Howell's *State Trials*, Volume 6, page 226, is a report of the trial of John Crook and others for refusing to take the Oaths of Allegiance and Supremacy. The sentence was:

> . . . you do incur a Praemunire, which is the forfeiture of all your real estate during life, and your personal estates for ever, and you to be out of the king's protection, and to be imprisoned during his pleasure; and this is your sentence.

While Jefferson once referred to Quakers as "Protestant Jesuits, implicitly devoted to the will of their superior,"[50] he thought kindly of them when writing:

> We should all, then, like the Quakers, live without an order of priests, moralise for ourselves, follow the oracle of conscience, and say nothing about what no man can understand, nor therefore believe; for I suppose belief to be the assent of the mind to an intelligible proposition.[51]

Chapter Six

PROSECUTIONS FOR SECULAR
AND MODERNISTIC SPEECH

In Thomas Jefferson's time, burnings for "heresy" had ceased, but imprisonments for alleged "blasphemy" had not. To preclude prosecutions in Virginia, Jefferson's Statute provided that "all men shall be free to profess, and by *argument* to maintain, their opinions in matters of religion [Italics author's]."

The term "argument" could have been suggested by the title of Dodwell's book, then extant, *Christianity Not Founded on Argument* (1742).

One of the things Jefferson's Statute prevented from occurring in Virginia, involving "opinions in matters of religion," took place in Pennsylvania in 1824. There a speaker in a debating society ventured to say: "The Holy Scriptures are a mere fable; they are a contradiction and although they contain a number of good things, yet they contain a great many lies."[1] The speaker was prosecuted and convicted under a statute as for the crime of blasphemy, and he was called a "malicious reviler of Christianity." The word "lies" was aggravating, and still is, which explains why heretical archbishops resort to the use of the term "myth."

The indictment of the Pennsylvania debater charged that the defendant's words were uttered "to the great dishonor of Almighty God, to the great scandal of the profession of the Christian, to the evil example of all others in like case offending." The Supreme Court itself added that a club like the one at which the defendant spoke would "qualify young men for the gallows and young women for the brothel." The same court ultimately became tolerant. In 1894 it treated respectfully and as legal the Friendship Liberal League.[2] The public itself became tolerant, for in 1914 the Pittsburgh Rationalist Society was unmolested, and on September 20th Marshall J. Gauvin lectured on "Mr. Noah and His Big Flood."[3]

Kentucky's early Constitution conformed to Jefferson's Statute. It was still in effect in 1894 when a trial judge quashed an indictment for "blasphemy" and declared:

> In a code of laws of a country enjoying absolute religious freedom there is no place for the common law crime of blasphemy. Unsuited to the spirit of the age, its enforcement would be in contravention of the constitution of this state, and this crime must be considered a stranger to the laws of Kentucky.[4]

New Jersey early had, and never repealed, its statute providing punishment for "any person who shall wilfully blaspheme the name of God."[5] An ex-Adventist and Unitarian, C. B. Reynolds, was prosecuted and convicted in 1887,[6] after a mob had wrecked his tent.[7]

New York did not trouble itself with the enactment of a statute, but used and kept its adopted common law, under which, in 1811, there was a prosecution and conviction of a man for having made some heterodox remarks about the parentage of Jesus.[8] The courts of that state took and followed as imperative authority the English decision of 1729 which held it to be the crime of blasphemy to say that the miracles ascribed to Christ ought to be taken allegorically only.[9] Jefferson was alluding to the New York case when he wrote:

> *Our* judges, too, have lent a ready hand to further these frauds, and have been willing to lay the yoke of their opinions on the necks of others; to extend the coercions of municipal law to the dogmas of their religion, by declaring that these make a part of the law of the land.[10]

As a reason for its decision, the highest court of New York said: "There is nothing in our manners or institutions which has prevented the application or the *necessity* of this part of the common law."

The state of Maine had and retained a blasphemy statute, and under it in 1921 one Mockus, a Socialist lecturer, was convicted because a translation of his lecture, delivered in the Lithuanian language, seemed to show ridicule of some biblical texts, including Mark 3:16, where it is written that Jesus "saw the spirit of God descending as a dove."[11] For the same lecture a conviction took place in the police court in Connecticut.[12]

(The temper of complainants in most cases was accordant with that of an ex-moderator of the Presbyterian General Assembly after he learned that Professor Miller of Princeton University opined that Jesus "was probably the son of Joseph and Mary." The cleric answered: "No crime more dastardly can be imagined than that of a teacher in a Christian university undermining the faith of the boys and girls of our Christian homes.")[13]

Mockus, convicted in Connecticut and in Maine, fared well in Illinois. There in 1917 an information against him was quashed on the basis of what the Illinois Supreme Court said in its 1910 school case, where it approvingly quoted from Jefferson's Preamble to the Virginia Statute, and declared: "The free enjoyment of religious worship includes freedom not to worship."[14] If Mockus had been proceeded against prior to 1910, he would have been convicted on the authority of the New York decision of 1811 and, more certainly, because of an Illinois decision of 1891 which denied to an indigent *agnostic* any relief from his suspension from the University of Illinois for nonattendance at chapel.[15]

The most famous blasphemy case in America was *Commonwealth of Massachusetts v. Abner Kneeland* in 1833, where the accused had merely published, without discussion, that he "did not believe in the God of the Universalists."[16]

Why eminent unbelievers were not prosecuted was explained by the Attorney General when prosecuting Henry Hetherington in 1841:

> Unfortunately there are to be found in some of the writings of these great authors [Rousseau, Hume, and Gibbon] passages unfavorable to revealed religion, but the great bulk of them may be perused with improvement, as well as with delight, by men of education and taste, to whom they are addressed, and who are capable of detecting errors and false reasonings intermixed with what is sound and salutary. The perusal of such works, upon the whole, is not pernicious, and an attempt to suppress them would be futile and ridiculous.[17]

Jurors were occasionally tolerant toward a popular defendant. At the third trial of William Hone in 1817 for his parody on the Litany, the jury acquitted him, even though they had been told by Lord Ellenborough that the parody was "a most impious and profane libel."[18]

The difference between lawful heresy and criminal blasphemy was indicated by the judge in the case against Samuel Waddington. The judge held him guilty because "he argues against the divinity of Christ by *denying the truth* of the Scriptures."[19] The defendant was charged with having published "maliciously," though he intended to inform, not injure, the public.

In 1842 George Jacob Holyoake was lecturing on economic matters, and in answering a question he said, briefly and candidly: "Morality I regard, but I do not believe there is such a thing as God." A lengthy and vituperative indictment followed. The judge said that the defendant's words had been "uttered in the heat of the moment." In his autobiography Holyoake wrote this about his leaving home for the trial:

My little daughter, Madeline, ran from her mother's knee to the door, when she found I had gone, and called after me down the street. Her sweet, clear voice arrested me. I looked back, and saw her dark, black eyes gleaming. I never met her glance again, nor heard her voice any more.[20]

Writing of his plight while in prison, he said:

Word was sent me that my child was ill, and then a letter came saying she was dead. . . . The sole income of home was from subscriptions from friends in various parts of the country. . . . A few days before the fever took the child, her mother was carrying her through Bull Street, Birmingham, when she cried from hunger for a bun in the window. There was no penny to buy it. . . .

Prosecutions for "blasphemy" were usually instigated by religionists of the victim's neighborhood, but after the imprisonment of Richard Carlile and wife in 1821 it was "the Great Duke" of Wellington who headed a public subscription "to prosecute Carlile's assistants."[21] One of them, John Clarke, was sentenced to three years' imprisonment, and to find securities for good behavior during life.[22] In Carlile's case the judge recognized the right to be heterodox secretly and silently, he saying:

The law of this country gives to every man the enjoyment of his own free opinions; it imposes upon no man articles of faith; each is left to himself to worship or not to worship, . . . and, as long as each man's opinion is *confined within his own breast*, the tribunals of this country have no right to make inquiry. But the offence . . . is not what you disbelieve, but that you have attempted to introduce disbelief into the minds of others, and to introduce disbelief to such an extent as to destroy the foundation of our future hopes.[23]

Carlile's "offence" was the sale of *Age of Reason.* Eight of his shopmen were imprisoned in 1824 for selling that book.

In the prosecution of Harry Boulter in London in 1908, the instructions to the jury were of such tenor as would redefine "blasphemy" as a crime only where the heterodox speech is "scurrilous," and made in circumstances inviting a "breach of the peace." Boulter was convicted for alleged scurrility in speeches on a street, where remarks "might even lead to a breach of the peace if hot, warm hearted believers pass by."[24] Thereafter Boulter spoke in a hall, and was not prosecuted.

Jefferson's Statute legalized "argument," regardless of its inclusion or exclusion of scurrility. He was familiar with English decisions in the Taylor (1676) and Woolston (1729) cases, which declared that "argument" and even unbelieving denials without argument were criminal.

Ernest F. Sterry in Toronto, Canada, in 1927 disparaged biblical stories of the Garden of Eden, and called Jehovah "this irate old party."[25] He was sentenced to sixty days in jail, the jury recommending deportation also. The judge legalized dissent if "couched in respectful terms."[26] In 1927 a man in Reading, Pennsylvania, was indicted for saying, when asked to put his hand on the Bible in taking an oath, "To hell with that."[27]

The blasphemy aimed at in the anti-evolution bills and statutes was at teachers only, and then only if teaching something inconsistent with *Genesis*. The Scopes trial resulted.

Aside from "blasphemy" laws, secularism had other obstacles. John M. Robertson observed:

> It is always to be remembered in regard to the struggle between Freethought and Religion that it is mainly a conflict between unsalaried and salaried combatants; between disinterested propaganda . . . and propaganda always backed by large vested interests. The latter . . . is on the side of an endowed institution, collectively rich, broad-bottomed on common prejudice, while the militant Freethinker appeals to the more thoughtful few, and is commonly poor, since the possession of wealth is a strong suasive to social conformity.

Secularists on trial could not speak freely, or were barred from freely speaking, in defense. When Thomas Tunbridge was prosecuted for selling Palmer's *Principles of Nature*, and was not allowed to read from the book, the judge (Abbott) afterward said: "I thought that a person on his trial for a libel on the Christian religion should not be allowed to make his defense a vehicle for the very crime for which he was answering."[28]

Jefferson had a copy of Palmer's book.[29]

Chapter Seven

PROSCRIPTIONS OF HERETICAL AND RATIONALISTIC PUBLICATIONS

Besides the criminal prosecutions, there are countless examples of legal and *extra*legal restraints upon heterodox publications. In 1819 a copyright was denied to Sir William Lawrence (1783-1867) for lectures on "physiology, zoology, and the natural history of man." The denial was on the ground that the lectures "impugned the doctrines of the immateriality and immortality of the soul," and "immortality of the soul is one of the doctrines of the Scriptures," and that "the law does not give protection to those who contradict the Scriptures."[1] The first lecture, in 1816, brought on the charge that Lawrence belonged to a party of French physiological skeptics aiming to "loosen those restraints on which the welfare of mankind depends."[2] Thereupon Lawrence replied in the next lecture, in 1817, and therein "discountenanced belief in immortality."[3]

In 1822 the protection of copyright was refused by the Court of Chancery to Byron's *Cain*.[4] What passages in *Cain* were blasphemous and unlawful are not quoted in any report of the case. In the drama, Cain refers to Abel's offer of a lamb, and says to Jehovah:

> If thou lov'st blood, the shepherd's shrine, which smokes
> On my right, hath shed it for thy service
> In the first of his flock, whose limbs now reek
> In sanguinary incense to thy skies. . . .

Then to Abel, Cain says:

> *His* pleasure! what was his pleasure in
> The fumes of scorching flesh and smoking blood,

63

> To the pain of the bleating mothers, which
> Still yearn for their dead offspring? or the pangs
> Of the sad ignorant victims underneath
> Thy pious knife? Giveway! this bloody record
> Shall not stand in the sun, to shame creation!

Byron must have thought, as Jefferson did, of "a blood-thirsty race, as cruel and remorseless as the Being whom they represented as the family god of Abraham, of Isaac and of Jacob, and the local god of Israel."[5]

The printing and publishing of a translation into English of Dr. Thomas Burnet's *Archaeologia Philosophica* (692) was, around 1816, enjoined by a Court of Chancery on the ground that it contained "reflections on religion" and ought, therefore, to be "concealed from the vulgar."[6] The original was in Latin, and was read by the clergy, not the poor ("the vulgar") and some clerical clamor was aroused against the author. One offending passage in Dr. Burnet's book was the following:

> We have . . . a very strange account of a serpent that talked with Eve, and enticed her to oppose God. I must confess, we have not yet known that this beast could ever speak, or utter any sort of voice, beside hissing. But what shall we think Eve knew of this business? If she had taken it for a dumb animal, the very speech of it would have so frightened her, that she would have fled from it. If, on the other side, the serpent had from the beginning been capable of talking and haranguing, and only lost his speech for the crime of having corrupted the faith of Eve, certainly Moses would have been far from passing over in silence this sort of punishment, and only mentioning the curse of licking the dust.

When Jefferson learned that his bookseller was threatened for procuring De Becourt's *Sur la Creation* he wrote:

I am really mortified to be told that, in the United States of America, a fact like this can become a subject of inquiry, and of criminal inquiry too, as an offense against religion; that a question about the sale of a book can be carried before the civil magistrate. Is this then our freedom of religion? and are we to have a censor whose imprimatur shall say what book may be sold, and what we may buy? And who is thus to dogmatize religious opinions for our citizens? Whose foot is to be the measure to which ours are all to be cut or stretched? Is a priest to be our inquisitor, or shall a layman, simple as ourselves, set up his reason as the rule for what we are to read, and what we must believe? It is an insult to our citizens to question whether they are rational beings or not, and blasphemy against religion to suppose it cannot stand the test of truth and reason. If M. de Becourt's book be false in its facts, disprove them; if false in its reasoning, refute it. But, for God's sake, let us freely hear both sides, if we choose.[7]

In 1841 Henry Hetherington was convicted for selling Haslam's *Letters to the Clergy*, and thereupon instigated a test prosecution of Edward Moxon (1801-58) for the sale of Shelley's works, which included *Queen Mab*, from which the indictment quoted:

> Is there a God?—Aye, an Almighty God,
> And vengeful as almighty! Once his voice
> Was heard on earth; earth shudder'd at the sound;
> The fiery-visaged firmament express'd
> Abhorrence, and the grave of nature yawn'd
> To swallow all the dauntless and the good
> That dared to hurl defiance at his throne,
> Girt as it was with power.[8]

And then charged:

> . . . thereby meaning and referring to the Scripture history of Korah, Dathen, and Abiram; and meaning that the said

Korah, Dathan, and Abiram, were dauntless and good, and were so dauntless and good for daring to hurl defiance at the throne of Almighty God.

The indictment also described Moxon as "an evil disposed and wicked person, disregarding the laws and religion of the realm."

The poem *Queen Mab* in the words "to swallow" was alluding to Numbers 16:32, "and the earth opened its mouth, and swallowed them up." Scholars say that the Book of Numbers is a composite of four independent and earlier narratives.[9]

History is replete with instances of book suppression. A cursory research might reach the suppression of the works of Eunomius,[10] the destruction of Emperor Julian's *Adversus Christianos*,[11] the burning of John Amos Comenius's *Historia Persecutionum* (1648),[12] the history and papers of Admiral Coligny destroyed at his assassination.[13] The Baptist "Primer" of the Reverend Keach, obscure and innocuous, was *publicly* burned.[14]

In 1766 a boy had a copy of Voltaire's *The Philosophical Dictionary* in his pocket "and was burned to death with the book in the streets of Paris." In 1908 a New York court held unenforceable a contract for the sale of that book, but the decision was reversed on appeal.[15]

Lecky says, ". . . Constantine ordered the destruction of the writings of the Arians when the Council of Nice had condemned them."[16] But it requires some gullibility to believe that Constantine's decree took the form reported in an ecclesiastical history as follows:

> If any treatise composed by Arius should be discovered, let it be consigned to the flames, in order that not only his depraved doctrine may be suppressed, but also that no memorial of him may be by any means left. This therefore I decree, that

if any one shall be detected in concealing a book compiled by
Arius, and shall not instantly bring it forward and burn it,
the penalty for this offense shall be death; for immediately
after conviction the criminal shall suffer capital punishment.[17]

Jefferson's concern regarding lost ancient books was shown
by his interest in the collection of J. A. Fabricius (1668-
1736).[18]

Publications not orthodox have been suppressed by private
individuals; for example, manuscripts which Anthony Collins
left for posthumous publication were destroyed by his
widow.[19] Benjamin Franklin's autobiography suffered a sub-
stitution for that passage in the original edition having the
words "the perusal of Shaftesbury and Collins made me a
sceptic."[20] Five volumes of John Toland (1670-1722) became irretrievably lost after his death.[21] Abraham Lincoln's
deistic manuscript was seized and burned by a friend.[22]

On the other hand, impostures in orthodox works did not
impede their circulation, for example, *Acta Sanctorum*, denounced by Adams[23] and by Jefferson.[24] It describes many
miracles, including those of St. Januarius,[25] and those of Saint
Helena.[26]

On September 25, 1895, a gift of Robert G. Ingersoll's
works was rejected by directors of the Farmington, New
Hampshire, library because, they said, "We do not wish to
alienate the affections of the founders and supporters of our
library, nor oppose the wishes of the best element of our
town." When Elbert Hubbard protested against a like re-
jection by the library board at East Aurora, New York, in
1908, he was answered, in part, by quotations from Jeremiah
S. Black, Ingersoll's bitter adversary.[27]

The proscribed works included the lecture *Foundations
of Faith*, which contained a paragraph of the "creed of science," which passage was read at Ingersoll's funeral, July

25, 1899. It was copied in *The New Age* of May, 1967, with the notation that the author is "unknown," and the passage taken from *Kleinknecht Encyclopedia*.

The library boards intended to protect the young, and they placed on open shelves David M. Nelson's *The Cause and Cure of Infidelity* (1836). Jefferson advised Peter Carr to "examine" the biblical story of Joshua and the sun. Nelson, on the other hand, advised his young readers:

> . . . if you will go to the opposer of Christianity. . . . Ask him what he thinks, when the Chinese history speaks of Yao, their king, declaring that in his reign the sun stood so long above the horizon that it was feared the world would have been set on fire; and fixes the reign of Yao at a given date, which corresponds with the age of Joshua the son of Nun.

Municipal libraries could not bar the eleventh edition of the *Encyclopaedia Britannica*. It contained the biographies and the histories of deism and of the higher criticism which secularists would like to popularize. The eleventh edition has been superseded by a new encyclopedia which omits much of the old material relating to "heresy," secularism, and the pre-Reformation persecutions. The biography of Edward Gibbon is greatly condensed. Some decades ago, books admired by rationalists, if placed on shelves, ultimately became mysteriously "lost." That was the fate, in some libraries, of Samuel P. Putnam's *400 Years of Freethought* and Albert Frost's *Popular Freethought in America*.

In August, 1918, a citizen gave to the Dover, New Jersey, library three books by John E. Remsburg: *The Bible, The Christ*, and *Six Historic Americans*. The Library Committee informed him that it "does not desire to place these books" upon their shelves. In 1940 the Free Public Library of Topeka, Kansas, rejected books by Theodore Schroeder, one being *A New Concept of Liberty*.

New England libraries would have rejected gifts of books

from the Jefferson library, which at one time contained Ethan Allen's *Reason the Only Oracle of Man,* and a book by Nicholas Antoine Boulanger (1722-59) denounced by the clergy in 1800 as "execrable." The name of every known atheistic and anti-religious author of the eighteenth century may now be found in the index to *Catalogue of the Library of Thomas Jefferson* (Library of Congress, 1953), *e.g.,* Baron d'Holbach (1723-89), Denis Diderot (1713-84), Baron Cloots (1755-94). One edition of Volney's *Ruins* was a translation begun by Jefferson. (*Catalogue,* II, 20.)

Chapter Eight

FALSE ASCRIPTIONS OF
''ILL TENDENCY'' TO
''INFIDEL'' ARGUMENT

"BREACH OF THE PEACE"

In the first prosecution in a temporal (not ecclesiastical) court, the offending words were: "Preaching is but prating; prayer once a day is more edifying." The judges then (1617) decided that their secular court had jurisdiction because the defendant's words "drew after them a temporal consequence, the disturbance of the peace."[1]

The Delaware court in 1839 declared its blasphemy statute necessary to placate "enraged" Christians because, in the absence of such a law, "it would be in vain to expect that a populace *enraged* by such means [anti-Christian utterances] could be restrained by being informed that the constitution protected him [the speaker]. That disgraceful law of the mob called 'Lynch Law' would, it is to be feared, be inflicted in spite of every effort to restrain them."[2]

In the Delaware case, the accused used provocative language in agreeing with what Jefferson called the "pretension" that Jesus "was a man of illegitimate birth."[3] The indictment against Thomas Jefferson Chandler alleged that he uttered "profane and blasphemous words . . . not having the fear of God before his eyes, but being moved and seduced by the instigation of the devil. . . ." At a later time the Supreme Court of North Carolina, too, recognized the seduction, stating that crimes are committed "from a perverse will brought about by the seductions of the evil one."[4]

In 1931 New York City denied a permit for public exposition of atheism, and a court said: "The passion, rancor, and

70

malice sometimes aroused by sectarian controversies and attacks on religion seem to justify especial supervision. . . ."[5]
When Virginia Baptist preachers were jailed, being pious, the
offense was not called "blasphemy," but they were accused of
breaking the peace.

In labor controversies, passion and rancor sometimes arise,
but the Supreme Court declared, in effect, that inflammatory
speech is free because it "may indeed serve its high purpose
when it induces a condition of unrest, . . . or even stir people
to anger."[6]

It might "stir" a cleric to "anger" if he heard Jefferson's
comment on a "hocus pocus of a God, like another Cerberus,
with one body and three heads."[7] The breach of the peace
is more likely to be incited by an interloper than by the
secularist speaker. When Harry Boulter was lecturing in
London, a religious paper quoted a part of the intruder's
language, some of which was:

> Can you listen unmoved to the manner in which that foul
> blackguard has assailed and scorned the stories which you have
> listened to from your dear mother's lips, to the pollution of
> those unspeakably tender truths which have solaced the weary
> and heavy laden, and which have brought comfort and con-
> solation to the dying ear in every part of the world for
> thousands of sorrow-laden years? Are you not filled with anger
> and wrath and indignation?[8]

Friends of Mr. Boulter could have read the following from
Jefferson:

> Ridicule is the only weapon which can be used against un-
> intelligible propositions. Ideas must be distinct before reason
> can act upon them; and no man ever had a distinct idea of the
> trinity. It is the mere Abracadabra of the mountebanks calling
> themselves the priests of Jesus. If it could be understood it
> would not answer their purpose. Their security is in their
> faculty of shedding darkness, like the scuttle-fish, thro' the

elements in which they move, and making it impenetrable to the eye of a pursuing enemy, and there they will skulk.[9]

With respect to "enthusiastic" sects, Lord Shaftesbury wrote to the same effect.[10]

Breaches of the peace have been committed by religionists down through history not only against atheists and "infidels" but also against such pious believers as were called "heretics." A historian dealing with the Council of Nicea, A.D. 325, writes: "When old Arius rose to speak, one Nicholas of Myra struck him in the face."[11]

William Black was killed in 1915 in Marshall, Texas, even before he rose to speak, and was yet in his hotel room. He intended to give an anticlerical lecture, which intent alone was enough to incite some Knights of Columbus.[12]

The Boston *Transcript* of April 4, 1916, reported that ten thousand rioters at Haverhill "were bent upon wreaking personal injury, possibly murder, upon the man who intended to speak at the City Hall." The man who, like Arius, rose to speak was Thomas F. Leyden, who had the support of local Protestant ministers.

The campus riots of 1969 aroused public clamor for punishment or prevention of interference with speech or speakers, but in the nineteenth century the preachers, politicians, and judges wanted to, and did, penalize the *speakers*, as if they, and not the assailants, were the criminals. After Elijah P. Lovejoy was murdered for defending his press, an attorney general approved the killing and said that Lovejoy had died "as the fool dieth."[13] "Dieth" was a biblical word.

DISSOLUTION OF THE CIVIL GOVERNMENT

On March 2, 1819, James Madison wrote to Robert Smith:

It was the universal opinion of the Century preceding the last, that Civil Government could not stand without the prop of a religious establishment, and that the Christian religion itself, would perish if not supported by a legal provision for its clergy. The experience of Virginia conspicuously corroborates the disproof of both opinions.[14]

It was in the seventeenth century that English judges said: ". . . that to say religion is a cheat is to dissolve all those obligations whereby civil societies are preserved." That was in 1676, and it was reported in 3 Keble's English Bench Reports, 607, which Jefferson cited on another aspect of Taylor's case.

It was in Woolston's case, 1729, that the judges first boldly proclaimed that to say that the miracles ascribed to Christ ought to be taken *allegorically* only "tends manifestly to a *dissolution* of the civil government."[15]

In 1756 it was alleged in an indictment of Jacob Ilive (1705-63) that his book contained "most impious and wicked opinions concerning the Truth of all revealed religion in general, to the *endangering* of the Public Peace, State, and *Government* of this Kingdom."[16]

The name of Peter Annet (1693-1769) was familiar to Jefferson, he having a copy of Annet's *History of the Man after God's Own Heart* (1761). Annet published nine issues of *The Free Inquirer* and was consequently accused of discrediting therein the Holy Scriptures, "particularly the Pentateuch." He may have discredited the story of Enoch's transit to heaven without having first died on earth (Genesis 5:24). The indictment against him recited, among other things, that he had "caused it to be believed . . . that the sacred truths and miracles recorded in the Pentateuch were impostures, . . . and thereby to . . . shake the foundations of the Christian religion, and of the *civil* and ecclesiastical *government* established in this kingdom."[17]

In Eaton's case, treated in Chapter II, the prosecutor considered anti-Trinity speech "an offense as serious to the well-being of society, as any that can be imagined."[18]

In 1728 the Grand Jury of Middlesex, England, brought out a verbose report, and among expressions therein were:

> So restless have these Zealots for Infidelity been in their diabolical Attempts against Religion, that they have,
>
> First, Openly blasphemed and denied the Doctrine of the ever-blessed Trinity, endeavoring by specious Pretences to revive the Arian Heresy, which was never introduc'd into any Nation, but the vengeance of Heaven pursu'd it.
>
> These Principles having a direct Tendency to the Subversion of all Religion and Civil Government.[19]

The Grand Jury presented each of five editions of Woolston's *A Discourse on the Miracles of our Saviour. . . .*

Thomas Paine's thesis was that his God did not commit the acts ascribed to Jehovah; yet the prosecutor cried out against the author of *Age of Reason:* "No man can be expected to be faithful to the authority of man who revolts against the government of God!"

Christians were fundamentalists in the eighteenth century, as were their judges, and naturally there was an alliance, even a fusion, of religion and government, but in 1920 the Supreme Court of Maine may have been too reactionary in saying: "*Stability* of government in no small measure depends upon the reverence and respect which a *nation* maintains toward its *prevalent* religion."[20] It is impossible for minority sects to have "reverence" for a prevalent sect. Naturally men *abhor* dogmas not their own, and Jefferson wrote "that to compel a man to furnish contributions of money for the propagation of opinions which he disbelieves and *abhors*, is sinful and tyrannical."

A researcher may be surprised to find that as late as 1886 an eminent Christian, in approving a then recent prosecution, said:

> . . . wherever, and wheresoever, and whenever, liberty of speech is incompatible with the safety of the state, liberty

of speech must fall back and give way, in order that the state may be preserved.[21]

He did not cite or quote any language which the accused had used. In Woolston's case, in 1729, the English court pointed out that what "tends manifestly to a dissolution of the civil government" was the defendant's assertion that the miracles ascribed to Christ ought to be taken allegorically only. Jefferson was familiar with that case, and others, and responded, in his Preamble, to the "ill tendency" dodge.[22]

What might endanger "safety of the state" was the legal doctrine of a Tennessee judge who would nullify that clause of the Tennessee Constitution, and a statute, which authorized divorces on grounds other than adultery, because such constitutional provision, and the statute, are contrary to biblical texts, including "what therefore God hath joined together, let no man put asunder."[23]

IMPAIRING EFFICACY OF OATHS

Early English law writers defined an oath as "a religious asseveration by which a person renounces the mercy and imprecates the vengeance of Heaven if he do not speak the truth." In 1685 Judge Jeffreys referred to the vengeance as "eternal flames" and "the bottomless lake of fire and brimstone." In 1797 a court declared the oath was made under "the dread of future punishment," and in 1799 a judge held a witness competent if believing the punishment may be "in this world or in the next." In any case the Bible was taken as the authority. Hence it was a crime to deny the truth of any biblical text because to create disbelief of one text might lead to disbelief of any passages relating to divine punishments.

In sentencing Thomas Williams for selling *Age of Reason,* Mr. Justice Ashhurst said:

Thomas Williams. You have been tried and found guilty of

publishing a most heinous and blasphemous libel, . . . tending to sap the foundation of our holy religion. . . .

Indeed, all offences of this kind are not only offences to God but crimes against the law of the land, and are punishable as such, inasmuch as they tend to destroy those obligations whereby civil society is bound together; and it is upon this ground that the Christian religion constitutes part of the law of England; but this law, without the means of enforcing its precepts, would be but a dead letter: Whenever those infamous works appear they are the proper subject of prosecution; for if the name of our Redeemer were suffered to be traduced, and his holy religion treated with contempt, the solemnity of an oath, on which the due administration of justice depends, would be destroyed, and the law be stripped of one of its principal sanctions, the dread of future punishments.[24]

Richard Price, Jefferson's English friend, would not have concurred in such an opinion. He had then written in the pamphlet *Importance of the American Revolution:*

All the experience of past time proves that the consequences of allowing civil power to judge of the nature and tendency of doctrines, must be making it a hindrance to the progress of truth, and an enemy to the improvement of the world.

At the trial of Mary Ann Carlile (1821) a judge said: ". . . it is upon religion that you and I administer justice. What is the obligation upon which we proceed? Upon the solemn sanction of an oath."[25]

In 1920 the Supreme Court of Maine made or recognized unbelief in biblical texts a crime when saying:

Shall we say that any word or deed which would rob official oaths of any of their sanctity, thus undermining the foundations of their binding force, would be protected by a constitutional religious freedom whose constitutional limitation is nondisturbance of the public peace? We register a *most emphatic negative.*[26]

When fear of hell was most prevalent, perjuries were "exceedingly common."[27] In 1926 there was "a widespread prevalence of perjury."[28] In 1927 "criminal justice" was "enmeshed in a web of perjury."[29] In 1933 there was "most shameless lying" by rival groups of trustees seeking control of church property.[30]

Lawyers after the eighteenth century did not trust the oath; hence the use of various tests of credibility, not involving religion, and cross-examinations. Judges of earlier times pretended to believe in the efficacy of even a pagan oath. In 1774 an English court said:

> Herod having sworn to Herodias that whatsoever she asked of him he would give it her, though he was exceeding sorry when she asked of him the head of Saint John the Baptist, yet for his oath's sake . . . he would not reject her.[31]

The biblical text alluded to goes on to say: "And straightway the king sent forth a soldier of his guard, and commanded to bring his head; and he went and beheaded him in the prison." Why was not Herod also afraid to commit that and other murders? A massacre of the children of Bethlehem is attributed to him.[32]

The same court also declared: ". . . no country can subsist a twelve-month where an oath is thought not binding; for the want of it must necessarily dissolve society."

Dean Wigmore told his law students that "there is much skepticism . . . about the effect and value of the oath."[33]

MORALITY AND HOPE OF HEAVEN

In 1821 Mary Ann Carlile's argument against the Messianic prophecies was denounced by the court for its tendency to shake "the faith upon which our *moral conduct* here, as well as our expectations of life hereafter, is built. . . ."[34] Her deism, being that of Thomas Paine and other English and American deists, has been superseded by the still more rationalistic Unitarianism, no longer accused of lessening "moral conduct."

Mary Ann's judge also said: "It has been stated that there are Jews who assert that Christ is not the Messiah. In their synagogues they may so assert. . . ."

Why may not secularists "so assert" in their own meeting place? It was in a debating club that a citizen in Pennsylvania asserted that the Holy Scriptures "contain a great many lies," and when the state's highest court upheld the conviction for blasphemy it further declared that such a club would become "a nursery of vice, a school of preparation to qualify young men for the gallows and young women for the *brothel*. . . ."[35] That statement, in 1824, was approvingly repeated by the same court in 1870.[36] Thereafter the "brothel" accusation never reappeared. Judge Charles B. Waite (1824-1909), one time judge in the Supreme Court of Utah, was unmolested when president of the American Secular Union in the early 1890's. In 1929-30 the respected mayor of Bradford, Pennsylvania, was president of the American Rationalist Association.[37]

It is common knowledge that Jefferson rejected every doctrine relating to the Trinity. Yet he could say:

> I have thought it better, by nourishing the good passions & controlling the bad, to merit an inheritance in a state of being of which I can know so little, and to trust for the future to him who has been so good for the past.[38]

Of several French atheists, he wrote that they "are known to have been the most virtuous of men."[39]

John Adams had no creed, and needed none, finding it enough to think as follows:

The faculties of our understanding are not adequate to penetrate the universe. Let us do our duty, which is to do as we would be done by; and that, one would think, could not be difficult, if we honestly aim at it.[40]

United States Senator Shelby M. Cullom in his *Fifty Years of Public Service* used the words: "From my reading of Scripture, and even admitting that there is a hereafter, I cannot find any satisfactory evidence to warrant such a belief."

In 1914 it was reported that Thomas E. Clemson, for whom Clemson Agricultural College (1889) was named, was an "atheist" and therefore the governor of South Carolina recommended a change of name to "Calhoun University."[41] Mark Twain was another "atheist."

Unbelievers began and kept their unbelief without any diminution of natural or earlier altruism. They could think of the orthodox dogmas, as did Jefferson when he wrote that "dogmas are made to interest our minds in the support of the teachers who inculcate them,"[42] and that "the Christian priesthood" had built up "an artificial system, which might . . . give employment to their order and introduce it to profit, power and preeminence."[43] His Preamble to the Bill for Establishing Religious Freedom hints that the priests were bribed by "worldly honours and emoluments."

Prison statistics relating to religion of the prisoners indicate that religion had no deterrent effect.[44] James Madison wrote:

If the impulse and the opportunity be suffered to coincide, we well know that neither moral nor *religious* motives can be relied on as an adequate control. They are not to be found to be such on the injustice and violence of individuals, and lose their efficacy in proportion to the number combined together, that is, in proportion as their efficacy becomes needful.[45]

John Adams noticed that ". . . religious terrors have little effect on Nations when they contradict a present passion, prejudice, imagination, enthusiasm or caprice."[46]

What "tendency" churchmen feared most was that the common people might agree with deistic or otherwise heterodox speakers, and desert the congregation. In 1797 the Proclamation Society was alarmed about the circulation of Paine's *Age of Reason*, and reported:

> In the beginning of the year 1796, the very excellent answer to it [*Age of Reason*] by a learned prelate, gave great hopes that the poison instilled into the minds of many of the readers would be converted to a wholesome and sober aliment, and the Society seemed to think that the noisome work would of itself die away; but they were disappointed: for at the close of that year, they were informed by many of their most intelligent members, who spoke from their own knowledge, that in several widely extended parts of the kingdom— . . . the work had been circulated with more than common industry, amongst considerable bodies of people, and was producing the most pernicious effects; and that new editions were preparing and about to be published in almost every part of the country.[47]

The book reached the common people in America too, and in 1800 the Reverend Mason wrote that Jefferson's friends "circulated with unremitting assiduity that execrable book of Boulanger" and also Paine's book.[48] In England there were imprisonments for republication of *Age of Reason* as late as 1824.[49]

The gnostic heretics, however sincere and peaceful, were once denounced as "servants of Satan, beasts in human shape, dealers in deadly poison, robbers and pirates."[50] What the Reverend Mason, Jefferson's adversary, thought of the contemporary heretics known as deists may be inferred from his comment on David Hume:

> He had, what rarely belongs to the ascertained infidel, a good

moral reputation. We mean that he was not addicted to lewd-
ness, to drunkenness, to knavery, to profane swearing, or any
of those grosser vices which are the natural and ordinary com-
panions of enmity to the gospel. . . .[51]

What the Reverend William Linn thought of deism, if it
spread among the common people, is inferable from this passage in his *Serious Considerations:* "Consider the effects
which the election of any man avowing the principles of
Mr. Jefferson would have upon our citizens. The effects
would be, to destroy religion, introduce immorality, and les-
sen all the bonds of society. . . ."
When in 1793, in Jefferson's home and in the presence
of Colonel John Trumbull, William Branch Giles expressed
an opinion that there is no "future state of existence, and
retribution for actions done here . . . ," Trumbull rejoined:

> Sir, in my opinion, the man who can with sincerity make the
> declaration which you have just made, is perfectly prepared for
> the commission of every atrocious action by which he can
> promise himself the advancement of his own interests. . . . Sir,
> I would not trust such a man with the honor of a wife, a sister,
> or a daughter—with my own purse or reputation, or with any-
> thing which I thought valuable. Our acquaintance, sir, is at
> an end.[52]

Trumbull's innuendo concerning dangers, from a Giles
atheist, to wife, sister, or daughter, reminds that the sociologist Professor Root concluded a paragraph thus:

> The close relationship between religion, sex and emotion is
> too well known to be discussed here, but suffice to say the most
> perfect cases of sordid sex offense and intense emotional re-
> ligious sincerity are to be found among those imprisoned for
> sex offenses.[53]

Mr. Justice Holmes was familiar with evangelical opinions

of atheists, and so interpolated into an opinion affecting
Rosika Schwimmer, an atheist, a statement that she was "a
woman of superior character and intelligence, obviously
more than ordinarily desirable as a citizen of the United
States."[54]

JEFFERSON'S ANSWER TO THE "ILL TENDENCY" ARGUMENT

Jefferson's opinion and intent are obvious from these
clauses in the Bill:

> . . . that the opinions and belief of men depend
> not on their own will, but follow involuntarily the
> evidence proposed to their minds;
>   that the opinions of men are not the object of
> civil government, nor under its jurisdiction;

Concerning the ecclesiastical assumption that heterodox
speech has an "ill tendency," he wrote in the Preamble:

> that to suffer the civil magistrate to intrude his powers into
> the field of opinion and to restrain the profession or propaga-
> tion of principles on supposition of their ill tendency is a
> dangerous fallacy, which at once destroys all religious liberty,
> because he being of course judge of that tendency will make
> his opinions the rule of judgment, and approve or condemn
> the sentiments of others only as they shall square with or differ
> from his own;

> that it is time enough for the rightful purposes of civil gov-
> ernment for its officers to interfere when principles break out
> into overt acts against peace and good order; and finally,

> that truth is great and will prevail if left to herself;

> that she is the proper and sufficient antagonist to error, and
> has nothing to fear from the conflict unless by human inter-
> position disarmed of her natural weapons, free argument and

debate; errors ceasing to be dangerous when it is permitted freely to contradict them.

The foregoing is, in effect, a restatement of what the Reverend Philip Furneaux wrote at greater length in *Letters to Blackstone* (1771). Passages therefrom appear in Appendix C.

When dissentient speech became more free, Cardinal Newman said, on May 17, 1879:

> Hitherto, it has been considered that religion alone, with its supernatural sanctions, was strong enough to secure the submission of the masses of the population to law and order. Now, philosophers and politicians are bent on satisfying this problem without the aid of Christianity.[55]

Jefferson once wrote:

> Subject opinion to coercion, and whom will you make your inquisitors? Fallible men, governed by bad passions, by private as well as public reasons.[56]

Even without bad passions or private reasons, Christian legislators, judges, and priests pretended to—and some did—believe that patriotism and religion would be impaired, and law and order weakened, by popular repudiation of the Mosaic miracle and other narratives. Hence the penalties imposed on Annet and the sellers of Paine's *Age of Reason*.

The "ill tendency" test has recently been revived in a form designated as the "balancing test" and was used against suspected "communists." Mr. Justice Black said:

> If I had ever doubted that the "balancing test" comes close to being a doctrine of governmental absolutism—that to "balance" an interest in individual liberty means almost inevitably to destroy that liberty—those doubts would have been dissi-

pated by this case. For this so-called "balancing test"—which, as applied to the First Amendment, means that the freedoms of speech, assembly, religion, and petition can be repressed whenever there is sufficient governmental interest in doing so —here proves pitifully and pathetically inadequate to cope with an invasion of individual liberty so plainly unjustified that even the majority apparently feels compelled expressly to disclaim "any view upon the wisdom of the State's action."[57]

Jefferson, Adams, and deists undoubtedly believed that convincing dissentient speech, if against *Trinitarian* doctrines, has no "ill tendency." Jefferson wrote to Adams:

If by *religion* we are to understand sectarian dogmas, in which no two of them agree, then your exclamation on that hypothesis is just, "that this would be the best of all possible worlds, if there were no religion in it."[58]

Chapter Nine

"CHRISTIANITY IS PARCEL OF THE LAW"

It was in Taylor's Case (1676) that Lord Hale first used this language: "Christianity is part of the laws of England, and to reproach the Christian religion is to speak in subversion of the law."[1] He did not say that, and he did not need to say it, in the earlier case of 1662 pertaining to witchcraft in which the penalty was hanging, for the *statute* made witchcraft a capital crime, and the "Holy Scriptures" were cited in proof of the actuality of witchcraft.

Hale's opinion in Taylor's Case was followed as imperative authority in Woolston's Case (1729), where the defendant's "reproach" was to publish that the miracles ascribed to Christ ought to be taken allegorically. Lord Raymond's language there was: "Christianity in general is parcel of the common law of England."[2]

Jefferson alluded to, or remembered, the foregoing cases when writing to Thomas Cooper on February 10, 1814:

> I promised you a sample from my commonplace book, of the pious disposition of the English judges, to connive at the frauds of the clergy, a disposition which has even rendered them faithful allies in practice.[3]

Archbishop Richard Whately (1787-1863) felt himself unable to determine the precise meaning of the "legal maxim" in question. Even if "Christianity" was part of the law, why could not one argue for the repeal of such law, or give information about other religions? In 1745 Elias de Paz, a Jew, thought it safe and legal to bequeath money for the maintenance of a place for instruction in the *Jewish* religion. But Lord Hardwicke held the bequest illegal, saying:

... the intent of the bequest was in contradiction to the Christian religion, which is part of the law of the land, which is so laid down by Lord Hale and Lord Raymond, and it undoubtedly is so.[4]

The bequest being illegal, it was nevertheless not allowed to revert to heirs, but one thousand pounds were given to the Foundling Hospital. There was such a hospital in London, founded in 1739, to reduce the number of newborn infants who were being thrown into the streets to perish.[5]

In the case against Henry Hetherington in 1841, Mr. Justice Patterson used this language:

... it is certain that the Christian religion is part of the law of the land ... it is impossible to say that the Old and New Testaments are not so intimately connected that if the one is true the other is true also; and the evidence of Christianity partly consists of the prophecies in the Old Testament.[6]

Lord Chief Justice Denman said "an attack upon the Old Testament ... is clearly indictable." So any part of the Christian religion was itself a "part of the law." And any biblical narrative was a part of the religion, and of the law, and by implication the law made it a crime to deny the literal truth of such narrative. Jefferson's Statute abrogated that part of the common law for Virginia.

More than a century and a half after Lord Hale launched the slogan, in 1822, Mrs. Susannah Wright, after conviction and when asked why punishment might be mitigated, proceeded to argue that Christianity was no part of the law of England, but Mr. Justice Bayley interrupted by saying: "... it is not *our* assertion, but the solemn decisions of *former judges*, that Christianity is parcel of the English law, and we cannot permit that point to be argued now."[7]

The Code of Alfred the Great was the first to receive a religious interpolation. Jefferson once observed:

... and I might go on further to show how some of the Anglo-Saxon priests interpolated into the text of Alfred's laws, the 20th, 21st, 22d, and 23d chapters of Exodus, and the 15th of the Acts of the Apostles, from the 23d to the 29th verses. ... What a conspiracy this, between church and state! ... rogues all; rogues all![8]

The object of the "conspiracy" was to compel popular adherence to the established church by making doctrinal dissent a crime called "heresy." When leading denominations became peacefully coexistent, unbelieving speech became the crime of "blasphemy."

Jefferson noticed one aspect of history when he said:

No historical fact is better established, than that the doctrine of one God, pure and uncompounded, was that of the early ages of Christianity, and was among the efficacious doctrines which gave it triumph over the polytheism of the ancients, sickened with the absurdities of their own theology. Nor was the unity of the Supreme Being ousted from the Christian creed by the force of reason, but by the sword of civil government, wielded at the will of the fanatic Athanasius. The hocus-pocus phantasm of a God like another cerberus, with one body and three heads, had its birth and growth in the blood of thousands and thousands of martyrs.[9]

Chapter Ten

CIVIL DISABILITIES FOR
NONCONFORMING THOUGHT
OR SPEECH

DISQUALIFYING NONBELIEVERS AS WITNESSES

In 1820 the highest court of New York, conforming to the English case of *Omichund v. Barker* as reported in 1 Atkyns 21, declared:

> By the law of England . . . it is fully and *clearly* settled, that infidels who do not believe in a God, or if they do, do not believe that he will either reward or punish them *in the world to come*, cannot be witnesses in *any* case, nor under any circumstances.[1]

"Punish" for what? For violation of the oath, it being a promise to the Deity. Not for injuries to persons. The English judge said:

> And I cannot help . . . to take notice of what is said by Lactantius on this subject, that some in his time, who were so very wicked as *not to be afraid* even of committing murder, yet had such a veneration for an oath and such a dread of being foresworn that when purged upon their oaths they durst not deny the fact.

Herod was not afraid to commit murder, but he was afraid to violate an oath even if the promise was to murder. The same English judge also said:

> Herod having sworn to Herodias that whatsoever she asked of him he would give it her, though he was exceeding sorry

88

when she asked of him the head of Saint John the Baptist, yet for his oath's sake . . . he would not reject her.

After the publication of the report by Atkyns, Chief Justice Willes modified the opinion by striking out the words "in the world to come" and substituting "in this world or in the next."[2]

Older than the Herod story is that of Jephthah, who "vowed a vow unto . . . whatsoever cometh forth from the doors of my house to meet me . . . I will offer it up for a burnt-offering."

Whatever the words of the oath mean, the witness could nevertheless silently tell his God that the audible words were *not* an actual vow. The lying witness then knew that if his falsehoods were discovered, he would be punished, if at all, only by the civil government. Titus Oates is infamous for his many perjuries. There are liars yet. In 1926 the American Bar Association was told:

The real and crying hindrance to a correct and efficient administration of justice lies in the widespread prevalence of perjury practiced with impunity by litigants and witnesses.[3]

The Supreme Court of North Carolina held it enough to believe only in divine punishments "in this world."[4] That interpretation qualified Jews, whose Old Testament "does not teach a future life."[5]

South Carolina required only belief "in the being of a God, and his providence."[6] Maryland, by Article 36 of its Constitution, disqualifies the unbeliever in divine punishments "in this world or the world to come."[7]

Jefferson thought of Connecticut as "the last retreat of monkish darkness, bigotry, and abhorrence of those advances of the mind which had carried the other states a century ahead of them."[8] Connecticut in 1828 conformed to the

Atkyns report of the 1744 *Omichund* case, holding a witness not competent without a belief in punishments "in the world to come."[9] When, thereafter, legislators favored abolition of requirement of that belief, a religious periodical maintained that to permit unbelievers to testify would convert the courts into "tremendous engines of oppression."[10]

In 1809 the judges there held that, if there is evidence that a proposed witness is an unbeliever, he cannot testify to the contrary, because, they said, "It would seem to be incongruous to admit a man to his oath for the purpose of learning from him whether he had the necessary qualifications to be sworn."[11]

The Supreme Court of Illinois in 1856 held an offering witness *incompetent* for lack of belief in divine punishments as was inferred from his statement:

> I am certain that there is an obligation on my part to tell the truth when sworn . . . I believe I should be responsible to the civil law if I should testify falsely; and, further, that I should be punished by losing the esteem of my fellow men. . . . I feel obligated to tell the truth aside from the actions of the civil law, and aside from what others may think of me.[12]

The court accepted that statement as truthful, as if he was competent to make it. So the common law, said to be accordant with "reason," presumed a witness truthful when avowing unbelief, but not trustworthy otherwise.

Colonel Ingersoll commented as follows:

> The supreme court of Illinois decided, in the year of grace 1856, that an unbeliever in the existence of an intelligent First Cause could not be allowed to testify in any court. His wife and children might have been murdered before his very face, and yet in the absence of other witnesses, the murderer could not have even been indicted. The atheist was a legal outcast. To him, Justice was not only blind, but deaf. . . . By such

infamous means has the Church endeavored to chain the human mind, and protect the majesty of her God.

The court intimated that it was less "inhuman" than Lord Coke was, for of him it said:

> In early times Lord Coke laid down the rule as excluding all not Christians—a rule as narrow, bigoted and inhuman as the spirit of fanatical intolerance and persecution which disgraced his age and country.

Coke has been quoted as follows:

> All infidels are, in law, perpetual enemies, . . . for between them, as with the Devil, whose subjects they be, and the Christians, there is perpetual hostility, and can be no peace.[13]

Coke's authority, cited by himself, was II Corinthians 6:15, "and what concord hath Christ with Belial?" In 1800 the Reverend John M. Mason cited that passage in his *Voice of Warning*, a pamphlet assailing Jefferson.

The third Constitution of Illinois went into operation August 8, 1870, and provided that "no person shall be denied any civil capacity . . . on account of his religious opinions." In Massachusetts the inclusion of the word "religious" would make a like clause inapplicable to atheists.[14] Jefferson would, as he did, remove ambiguity with the phrase "opinions in matters of religion."

Jefferson in *Notes on Virginia* observed that "constraint may make him [the proscribed witness] worse by making him a hypocrite, but it will never make him a truer man." The witnesses most likely to be asked religious questions were those of an unpopular minority, as in the case of John Most, anarchist.[15] However, the inquisition was encouraged by this declaration of a court:

... [unbelief] shows a recklessness of moral character and utter want of moral sensibility, such as very little entitles him to be heard or *believed* in a court of justice sitting in a country designated as Christian.[16]

The judges never explained the time, place, nature, and duration of the divine punishment for perjury, or the effect of confession, absolution, or deathbed repentance. The famous Christian judge, Baron Jeffreys, told a witness:

Consider that the Great God of Heaven and Earth . . . will call thee to an account for the rescinding His truth, and take vengeance of thee for every falsehood thou tellest. I charge thee, therefore, . . . that thou do not dare to waver one tittle from the truth, . . . for that God of Heaven may justly strike thee into eternal flames and make thee drop into the bottomless lake of fire and brimstone, if thou offer to deviate the least from the truth and nothing but the truth.[17]

The judge was conforming to Revelation 21:8:

But for the . . . unbelieving, . . . and all liars, their part shall be in the lake that burneth with fire and brimstone; which is the second death.

A Negro citizen could be both believing and truthful, yet the Ohio legislature once enacted:

. . . no black or mulatto person shall be permitted to be sworn or give evidence . . . in any prosecution . . . against any white person.[18]

Mr. Justice Samuel Chase yearned for a chance to impute atheism to Jefferson and disqualify him as a witness if and when he would appear as such. In 1800 James Monroe informed Jefferson as follows:

Chase harangued the G. Jury in a speech said to be drawn with some art, as it inculcated some popular doctrines with allusions which, supported by Eastern calumnies, he *intended for you*. He declared solemnly he would not allow an atheist to give testimony in court.[19]

The General Court of Virginia in 1846 approbated Jefferson's Statute by noting that under the common law, operative before the enactment of the statute,

The proscribed man may suffer in his property, or in the persons of the members of his family. His goods may be stolen, his dwelling broken into by the midnight robber, or burned by the incendiary; his child may be beaten, or his wife murdered before his face, and the offender escape because of the incapacity of the injured man to give evidence against him. This very incapacity may have caused the calamity.[20]

The witness rejected for his secularism was usually not one of the litigants and therefore could not appeal and have a ruling on his disqualification published in the law reports. Only a local newspaper would mention his exclusion, as where in 1925 in Union County, Arkansas, Dr. W. T. Carter, a state's witness, was barred because of nonbelief in "a Christian God." Ten years earlier, in Pulaski County, in a libel case, E. W. Perrin was rejected as a witness. Such cases were rare because a witness is presumed to be competent, and there is no religious inquisition. However, a "Socialist" would sometimes be questioned for purpose of harassment, it being known that Socialists like Upton Sinclair or Robert Dale Owen abhorred religious as well as economic oppressions.

In 1929 in Rockville, Maryland, the victim of a theft was barred from testifying against the alleged thief because he, the complainant and witness, did not believe in God or "future punishment for sin." The State's Attorney then confessed to a plea of not guilty, and there was no appeal. The *Washington Evening Star* reported the case, and a reader could assume that a religious thief in Maryland has the "liberty" and the *license* to steal from an atheist.

In 1829 Thomas Herttell's *The Demurrer*, which opposed the religious test, was denounced in an editorial which assumed that *absence* of religious belief would indicate "renunciation of moral obligation."[21] If *presence* of orthodox belief insures the moral obligation, then instead of an oath it ought to be enough that a witness is a believer and the oath be omitted. A federal judge seemed to think so when suggesting, after a priest came to the stand, "that the formality of the oath be waived."[22]

Some of the early New England judges must have thought that the secularist (then called "infidel") is apt to be untruthful because, as a result of the "original sin," men are naturally "made opposite to all good, and wholly inclined to all evil."[23]

In 1789, in an eastern federal court, one Emmons was not permitted to testify against the thief who had stolen his goods. Emmons's belief did not go further than "Nature to be God, and God to be Nature, and in him we live and move and have our being."[24] The federal rules now provide: ". . . competency of witnesses shall be governed . . . by the principles of the common law as they may be interpreted . . . in the light of reason and experience." A witness not believing in the "God of the Bible" is competent.[25]

In February, 1931, the following was reported in a magazine:

> In Newark, New Jersey, Judge —— of the Essex County Court of Quarter Sessions recently refused in . . . 1930 to let seven proffered witnesses testify in behalf of Dozier W. Graham . . . , charged with inciting a riot, holding that they were incompetent because they did not believe in God. And Graham has been convicted and faces a sentence of imprisonment.[26]

Nonreligious witnesses in England suffered as in America, but were finally freed by the Oaths Act of 1888, which provided:

> . . . every person upon objecting to being sworn, and stating, as the ground of such objection, either that he has no religious belief, or that the taking of an oath is contrary to his religious belief, shall be permitted to make his solemn affirmation instead of taking an oath in all places and for all purposes where an oath is or shall be required by law, which affirmation shall be of the same force and effect as if he had taken the oath. . . .[27]

It is generally assumed that state constitutions have uniformly removed or modified common law disabilities of the nonreligious, but Section 2, Article VII, of the 1836 Constitution of Arkansas provided: "No person who denies the being of a God shall hold any office in the civil government of this State, *nor be allowed his oath* in any court." This was repeated in the Constitution of 1864. The next Constitution (1874) provided that "oaths or affirmations" shall not be "dispensed with." A like provision in the Ohio Constitution was construed as requiring, as under the common law, "a belief in a supreme being, who will certainly, either in this life or in the life to come, punish perjury."[28]

A statute permitting affirmations in place of oaths could still keep the atheist incompetent. Writing in 1929 in *The North Carolina Law Review* a one-time judge quotes the North Carolina form of affirmation as follows:

> I, —— do appeal to God, as a witness of the truth and the avenger of falsehood, as I shall answer the same at the great day of judgment, when the secrets of all hearts shall be known.

As a declaration of public opinion, or policy, the North Carolina legislature in 1777 declared:

Whereas lawful oaths for the discovery of truth and establishing rights are necessary and highly conducive to the important end of good government; and being most solemn appeals to Almighty God, as the omniscient witness of truth and
the just and omnipotent avenger of falsehood, such oaths,
therefore, ought to be taken and administered with the utmost
solemnity.[29]

A long section includes a provision that the witness "shall
kiss the Holy Gospel...."

IMPEACHMENT OF CREDIBILITY

Jefferson's Statute provided that a man's "religious opinions
or belief" shall in no wise "diminish" his civil capacities. At
common law the civil capacity to be a witness was not merely
diminished but taken away entirely from a man not believing there are "divine" punishments. Finally some courts and
legislatures began to substitute the "impeachment" rule, expressed in one statute as follows: "Facts which have hereto-
fore caused the exclusion of testimony may still be shown
for the purpose of lessening its credibility."[30] Such statutes
were passed as "a sop of mediaevalism left to satisfy those
who would otherwise not have consented to abolish theological qualifications for the oath."[31] The impeachment was still
a religious inquisition conducted in the expectation that the
jury might disbelieve a witness having no fear of divine
punishments for perjury, or pretend to disbelieve simply to
hurt the "infidel." An English judge made the understate-
ment: "Unbelief acts prejudicially against a man."[32]

"Unbelief" may relate to any one of many doctrines. Proving a witness to have unbelief is intended to make a religious
jury disbelieve that witness. In 1829 it was the public opinion
in Connecticut that unbelief in "future retribution" causes
"renunciation of moral obligation" to tell the truth when on
the witness stand, and that "the possessor of such a creed
[of unbelief], if exposed, will be regarded with universal

horror and indignation."[33] It was Jehovah, not the "one God" of the deists, to whom the New Hampshire judges referred when declaring: "He who openly and deliberately avows he has no belief in the existence of a God, . . . is *unworthy of any credit* in a court of justice."[34]

Jurors would be inclined to attribute unbelief to a witness simply because he was questioned about his belief. A North Carolina judge permitted such questions, and said: "If I believed that life ends with death, and that there is no punishment after death, I would be less apt to tell the truth."[35]

In 1913 a New York magistrate discharged a prisoner accused of theft because the people's witness was either incompetent or unbelievable in the opinion of that judge. The witness, a boy aged eleven, had been asked what would happen to him if he told a lie, and he replied "I don't know." To the prisoner, the judge thereafter said:

> You ought to be very thankful for the inefficient public school system of this city for your discharge. Certainly it is a sad commentary on the system when a boy nearly twelve years old is unable to answer the question I've asked.[36]

The "question" did not allude to any crime or statute relating to perjury but to "what would happen" according to orthodox religious teachings on divine "punishments."

Adult Christian witnesses escaped impeachments, and a Catholic witness could not be asked whether his belief in confession and absolution is being thought of when testifying.[37]

Repeals of statutes permitting religious impeachment of witnesses were long delayed. In 1884 Senator John F. Andrew, son of the war governor John A. Andrew, sought, without success, to secure such repeal in Massachusetts.[38]

In 1846 the New York Constitution was so amended as to abolish the common law disqualification of unbelieving witnesses, and provided: "No person shall be rendered incompetent to be a witness on account of his opinions of matters of religious belief." But the impeachment was not prohibited, and so in 1891 the Court of Appeals upheld impeachment of an unpopular "anarchist," John Most.[39] However, in 1903 the impeached witness was a respected citizen, and the court then held that impeachment on religious grounds cannot be allowed.[40]

Pennsylvania in 1909 enacted a statute forbidding both disqualification and impeachment of a witness on account of "opinions on matters of religion" or "religious belief."[41] That fact was not popularly known, and in 1923 a lawyer attempted to impeach John G. Palmer, if not also to disqualify him, as if only the common law was in effect. But Mr. Palmer, of Greencastle, Pennsylvania, knew of, and successfully invoked, that statute.

EXCLUDING OR IMPEACHING DYING DECLARATIONS

In New Jersey in 1857 a man was found stabbed in the throat and bleeding so profusely that death was imminent. He identified his assailant. At the trial of the killer the jury was instructed that, if the deceased had no belief "in a future state of rewards and punishments," it must *disregard* the dying declaration.[42]

In Missouri two sons found their father dying from wounds inflicted by assailants whom he identified. At the trial the accused offered to prove that the deceased was "a disbeliever in God and in a future state of man." The Supreme Court of Missouri held that such proof *ought* to have been received,[43] citing cases, including one where the Supreme Court of the United States said: ". . . dying declarations . . . may be *discredited* by proof that he did not believe in a future state of rewards and punishments."[44] The "proof" would be a public stigmatization of the deceased, and thus augment the sufferings of the bereaved family.

The Supreme Court of Mississippi would *exclude* the dying declaration of an "infidel,"[45] which term could mean a pagan, an agnostic, a Jew, or a Mohammedan. An editorial on the Mississippi decision stated:

> The state, in prosecuting Gambrell, assumes that despite his belief he may have committed a murder, and also that despite the fact that he is a murderer he will tell the truth—that a man who is capable of committing murder is incapable of lying! The victim has no fear of eternity because he does not believe in a future life; the murderer fears eternity but knows that by repentance the occasion for fear will be removed, and if he perjures himself he has the same remedy. Why, then, should he hesitate at crime and perjury because of the future?[46]

Of course the American judges thought they were accordant with "precedent." In an early English case two persons were indicted for the murder of a child aged four by beating on the head. Shortly before her death, the child made a statement to her mother as to the manner in which she had been treated by the two prisoners. The court would not allow the declaration to be admitted, for the reason that the statement did not show that the child "had any idea of a future state."[47]

The Fourteenth Amendment to the United States Constitution, granting to "all persons . . . the equal protection of the laws," was ratified in 1868. Yet courts of many states, and the Supreme Court, continued to legalize exclusion or impeachment of dying declarations of some persons. The Supreme Court of Oregon in 1911 refused to make such a ruling,[48] and was criticized by the *Harvard Law Review* for so doing.[49]

Where either the New Jersey or the federal rule prevailed, a murderer-defendant had two advantages: (a) the victim, being dead, could not refute the killer's testimony on unbelief; and (b) even if the jury believed the dying declaration, it would free the accused if one juror voted for acquittal because of hatred for "infidels" generally. Connecticut judges once said: "It [unbelief] can scarcely fail to deprive him of the esteem of mankind, exclude him from intercourse with men of piety and virtue, and render him odious and detestable."[50]

Dr. Harry Elmer Barnes, sociologist, quoted with approval in 1931 the following from *Journal of Criminal Law and Criminology:*

> The time will eventually arrive when the dying victim of a brutal murder, in naming his assailants, will not be stigmatized and have his dying declaration discredited in court merely because he disbelieved in hell as described by orthodox Christians in the seventeenth century.[51]

EXCLUDING TESTIMONY OF CHILDREN

Of the testimony of "a little girl nine years of age" a school *Fourth Reader* says:

> She told her story with the simplicity of a child, as she was, but there was a directness about it which carried conviction of its truth to every heart. She was rigidly cross-examined. The counsel plied her with many and ingenious questionings, but she varied from her first statement in nothing.
>
> The truth as spoken by that little child was sublime. Falsehood and perjury had gone before her testimony. The prisoner had intrenched himself in lies, until he deemed himself safe. But before her testimony falsehood was scattered like chaff.[52]

The Supreme Court of Alabama reversed a conviction of rape because the nine-year-old witness "showed no such religious training and instruction as excited a hope of future reward to the good and fear of punishment to the wicked."[53] The court thus conformed to an English decision of 1829 in a case where two ruffians were indicted for murder of a four-year-old child by beating on the head. The court excluded evidence of the child's dying declaration about by whom and how the assault was committed. The exclusion was based on absence of proof that the child "had any idea of a future state."[54]

In Alabama, again, a boy of fourteen was held incompetent because he said: "I do not know what will become of me when I die, if I swear to a lie."[55]

Parents were advised to catechize a prospective child witness. So a court permitted a child to testify where: "She said . . . that *they* told her before she was summoned as a witness . . . that she was sworn to tell the truth; that if she would tell the truth, and be good, she would go to Jesus when she died."[56]

In 1904 a Louisiana court declared it "would amount to a travesty of justice" to exclude evidence of children who were not taught "about God or Heaven" where their testimony is necessary for proving the guilt of one committing a crime against *them*.[57] Why not also where the crime is against someone else?

DEPRIVING SECULARISTS OF CUSTODY OF CHILDREN

The poet Shelley was denied custody of his children on the ground that he "derided the truth of the Christian revelation."[58] In 1878 Annie Besant was deprived of her daughter, after pleading that bringing up Emily without religious indoctrination would hurt no one, and that "Mr. John Stuart Mill was brought up in this manner by his father, and no injury to his character resulted."[59] The judge, Sir George Jessel, said: "I think such a course of education not only reprehensible but detestable, and likely to work utter ruin to the child."

On June 10, 1878, Colonel Robert G. Ingersoll wrote to Mrs. Besant: "A few moments ago I read an account of the proceedings in Court when your child was torn from your arms by a robed brute acting as an English judge. . . . There is no language strong enough to express my hatred of Sir George Jessel and my sympathy for you.[60]

Mrs. Besant's appeal to a higher court was dismissed, the justices pretending to fear that if Emily "were allowed to remain with the mother, it is possible, and, perhaps, not improbable, that she would grow up to be the writer and publisher of such works as those [Mrs. Besant's] before us."

The legalized abduction of Emily was accomplished by force. Still weak from scarlet fever, the child was carried away shrieking and struggling, frantic with fear. Mrs. Besant wrote in her autobiography:

> The loneliness and silence of the house, of which my darling had always been the sunshine and the music, weighted on me like an evil dream; I listened for the patter of dancing feet, and merry thrilling laughter that rang through the garden, the sweet music of the childish voice; during my sleepless nights I missed in the darkness the soft breathing of the little child; each morning I longed in vain for the clinging arms and soft, sweet kisses. At last health broke down, and fever struck me, and mercifully gave me the rest of pain and delirium instead of the agony of conscious loss.

English deists who were parents abstained from public expression of their opinions. They were subject to the Act of 9 William III, c. 32 (1698), which was copied and adopted in Virginia in 1705. Jefferson took notice of it when he wrote:

> By our own Act of Assembly of 1705, if a person brought up in the Christian religion denies . . . the Trinity . . . or denies . . . the Scriptures to be of divine authority, he is punishable by . . . disability to be guardian. . . .
>
> A father's right to the custody of his own children being founded in law on his right of guardianship, this being taken

away, they may of course be severed from him and put by the authority of the court into more orthodox hands.[61]

In 1870 a religionist sought to remove a testamentary guardian because the latter was "an infidel of . . . Universalists, who deny the gospel. . . ." The court denied the removal.[62] In 1925 another Christian sought to prevent the appointment of Rupert Hughes as guardian of a minor because Hughes was author of *Why I Quit Going to Church*.[63]

In 1817 Jefferson denounced a proposed statute in New York which, if enacted and enforced, would take away from "Shaking Quakers" all their children and property, and "carry us back to the times of darkest bigotry and barbarism, to find a parallel."[64]

To deprive a secularist mother of custody of a child it was possible to resort to the device of *adding* evidence of matters not relating to religion, so that a court could say there were "proofs, *apart* from the many irrelevant beliefs of the wife"[65] or mother.

In recent times Pennsylvania had a statute providing that "persons of the same religious persuasion as the parents of the minor are *preferred* as guardians." A Presbyterian Confession of Faith had an article requiring that such Christians "as profess the true reformed religion should not marry with infidels, papists, and other idolaters. . . ." The Solemnization of Marriage Act of Nova Scotia once authorized *only* ministers of a church or officers of the Salvation Army to perform the ceremony. Where no law is involved, or any right, the Connecticut court informed that the "infidel" is "odious and detestable."[66] So to avoid any of the many forms of persecution, the "infidel" maintained silence, and attended religious formalities. He was beset with coercions. Jefferson wrote: "What has been the effect of coercion? To make one half the world fools, and the other half hypocrites; to support roguery and error all over the earth."[67]

Even some *divorce* cases reveal the thinking of a fundamentalist judge. In 1916 the Butte, Montana, *Miner* purported to quote a judge and a divorce plaintiff. The latter concluded her testimony by saying: "I never saw my husband kneel or offer a prayer." The judge then said: "Very well, I will sign your decree. I have no use for a man who never prays."[68]

One judge, as a lone dissenter, in *Lanier v. Lanier*, reported in Volume 5 of Heiskell's Tennessee Reports, voted to dismiss a bill for divorce because the statute which authorized divorce on the grounds on which plaintiff relied was contrary to verses 3 to 10 inclusive of the 19th chapter of Matthew. In the long opinion of the judge, the following passages appear:

> Every lawyer in the land has been taught not only that the Bible *is law*, but that it is the source of law.
>
> • • • • • • • • • • • •
>
> The law discredits the infidel. All these things are so because the Bible is the supreme law. . . . Thus we acknowledge it as the foundation of all law, which must be consistent with and conform to it, otherwise it is no law.

The framers of the Constitution of the United States took care to provide that it, and laws in pursuance thereof, "shall be the *supreme* law of the land. . . ." Under that section (2 of Article VI) the Bible is neither the supreme nor any other "law."

BARRING UNBELIEVERS FROM PUBLIC OFFICE

Charles Bradlaugh was several times elected to Parliament, but for a long time he was denied the right to act as a member, simply because of legal incapacity to make oath, especially oath of office.[69]

The English Act of 1698 (9 William III, c. 32) provided, among other things:

> ... that if any person or persons having been educated in, or at any time having made any profession of, the Christian religion . . . shall, by writing . . . or advised speaking deny any one of the persons in the Holy Trinity to be God . . . or shall deny the Christian religion to be true, or the Holy Scriptures of the Old and New Testament to be of divine authority, and shall . . . be . . . convicted, . . . such person or persons for the first offence shall be adjudged incapable and disabled in law . . . to have or enjoy any office or offices, . . . And if any person . . . so convicted . . . shall at the time . . . enjoy or possess any office, . . . such office . . . shall be void, and is hereby declared void.

The Act of 1698 was copied and adopted in Virginia in 1705. Its existence prompted Jefferson to include in his Resolution of 1776 in the House of Delegates the following:

> ... that ... every act ... either of the Parliament ... or of Great Britain . . . which renders criminal the maintaining of any opinion in matters of religion, . . . or which prescribes punishments for the same, ought to be declared henceforth as of no validity or force within this commonwealth.[70]

Civil rights include the right to hold public office, as Jefferson observed in the Preamble:

> ... that our civil rights have no dependence on our religious opinions, . . . and therefore the proscribing any citizen as unworthy the public confidence by laying upon him an incapacity of being called to offices of trust or emolument, unless he profess or renounce this or that *religious opinion*, is depriving him injudiciously of those privileges and advantages to which, in common with his fellow-citizens, he has a natural right. . . .

In the Bill of Rights in the Kentucky Constitution of 1891, it is provided that "the civil rights, privileges or capacities of no person shall be taken away, or in any wise diminished or enlarged, on account of his belief or *disbelief* of any religious tenet, dogma or teaching."

In Colorado "no person shall be denied any civil or political right, . . . on account of his opinions concerning religion," but the Constitution also requires "every civil officer" to "take and subscribe an oath or affirmation," and the statute permits an affirmation only where there are "conscientious scruples against taking an oath." An Alabama court held:

> The adoption of an "affirmation" as a substitute for the oath was adopted, not as a relaxation of the rule requiring a belief in a Supreme Being, but in recognition of those who, believing, conscientiously believe also that the divine command is to "Swear not at all."[71]

The Constitution of Ohio forbids religious tests, except that, as in Colorado, "nothing herein shall be construed to dispense with oaths and affirmations." An Ohio court said that one cannot make oath unless he has his moral nature strengthened by a belief in a Supreme Being "who will certainly, either in this life or in the life to come, punish perjury."[72] So the question arises whether one lacking that kind of "belief" can, if challenged, hold office either in Ohio or Colorado, or any other state requiring "oaths and affirmations."

A North Carolina court said that "the old Scriptures, which is the Hebrew Bible, does not teach a future life, and hence there is absent therefrom the doctrine of *future* rewards and punishments." So how could a Jew hold office in North Carolina?

The 1835 Constitution of Tennessee provides:

No person who denies the being of a God, or a future state of rewards and punishments, shall hold any office in the civil government of this state.

And a judge said:

Why, it may be asked. It is answered, because he cannot take an oath—he cannot be trusted. . . . The constitution has pointed her artillery against such as avow themselves to be atheists. No law can place an atheist upon a footing with a Christian. . . .[73]

The 1776 Constitution of North Carolina provided:

No person who shall deny the being of God, or the truth of the Protestant religion, or the divine authority of the Old or New Testament or who shall hold religious principles incompatible with the freedom and safety of the State, shall be capable of holding any office or place of trust or profit in the civil department within this state.

Notwithstanding that provision, in 1833 a Catholic, William Gaston, became a member of the Supreme Court. In deference to him, and to Catholics generally, in 1835 the North Carolina Constitution was amended to substitute the word "Christian" in place of "Protestant."

The Constitution of Georgia was at first modeled after the 1776 Constitution of North Carolina, using the phrase "Protestant religion," probably because the colony was founded as a refuge for persecuted Protestants as well as indigent classes.

In 1868 the Constitution of North Carolina was made to read: "The following classes of persons shall be disqualified for office: First. All persons who shall deny the existence of Almighty God. . . ." The state's Supreme Court later had occasion to say that a juror is disqualified "if he be an atheist. . . ."[74]

The Wilmington, North Carolina, *Star* of February 6, 1922, reported that, after a prospective juror said he did not "believe there is a God," the judge told him: "You are excused. You are not fit to serve on a jury." In *Georgia*, such a juror would be competent, for a citizen of Barnesville, Georgia, reported, December 12, 1925, that an "atheist" was elected Justice of the Peace after being repeatedly called an "atheist" during the campaign.

The Constitution of Delaware of 1776 prescribed a form of oath of office which recited a profession of "faith" in the Trinitarian doctrines there specified,[75] but the Pennsylvania Constitution of 1776 required only "a belief in God, the Creator and Governor of the universe, the rewarder of the good and the punisher of the wicked." That was deism, and Benjamin Franklin was president of the constitutional convention.

The Maryland Declaration of Rights required of all public officers "a declaration of belief in the existence of God." On June 19, 1961, the Supreme Court of the United States held that no officer can be excluded from office for failure to make that declaration.[76]

Connecticut, "the last retreat of monkish darkness,"[77] needed no law to bar "infidels" from public office, for public opinion would proscribe even a heterodox Christian, the highest court once declaring: ". . . it [infidelity] can scarcely fail to deprive him [infidel] of the esteem of mankind, . . . and render him odious and detestable."[78] In 1829 a New Haven magazine asserted that a nonbeliever in divine punishments after death is "destitute of all sense of moral obligation."[79]

When Catholics were barred from public office in England under Test Acts, there were protests from non-Catholics. The Irish Presbyterian John Abernethy (1680-1740) was "against all laws that, upon account of mere differences of religious opinions and forms of worship, excluded men of integrity and ability from serving their country."[80] But his grandson (John Abernethy, 1764-1831) is remembered chiefly for his "foul attack" upon Professor William Lawrence (1783-1867) for the lectures in physiology which were thought to be contrary to "the Scriptures."[81]

With no thought of the Constitution, there is religious opposition to a candidate because of sectarian affiliations of either the candidate or the voter, as where, in 1908, the Reverend H. C. Morrison published, against Judge Howard Taft, then an aspirant to the presidency, an article entitled: "A Horrifying Proposition Before the American People."[82] A fellow Republican said: "All the money in the world could not induce me to vote for a man for President who does not believe in Jesus Christ."[83]

In England, in 1606, by the statute of 3 James I, c. 5, "papists" were disqualified from any public office, from being executors, or from being guardians of children.[84] The United States Constitution forbids any federal officer to accept any present or title "from any king, prince or foreign state." Because some people regarded the Pope as a king or prince and the Vatican a "foreign state," a United States district judge declined a proffered Knight Commandership in the Order of St. Gregory.[85]

Jefferson's Statute provided that "civil capacities" of "no man" shall be diminished on account of opinions, meaning to protect not only state officers but also all employees of any governmental agency. Accordant with that was the Texas statute which provided that "no religious qualification shall be required for admission to any office or privilege in the university [of Texas]. . . ." But, contrary to that statute, and to Jefferson's principle, in 1923 the regents of that university issued a resolution to the effect "that no Infidel, Atheist or Agnostic be employed in any capacity in the University of

Texas."[86] Private sectarian colleges still adhere to such a policy, and some have discharged professors for opinions still religious but thought to be heretical.[87]

Neither the public nor any individual would have suffered any loss or damage if "atheists" and theists having no belief in divine punishments had been eligible for public office. In France the atheist Georges Clemenceau (1841-1929) served his country long and well. In Italy the atheist Ernesto Nathan (1845-1924) was elected mayor of Rome by an aldermanic vote of 60 to 12, and served competently. In Japan the atheist Baron Dr. Hiroyuki Kato was respected as privy councillor, president of Tokio Imperial University, and tutor to the emperor's father.[88] In India the people appreciated the services of Mahatma Virchand Raghavji Gandhi, B.A., M.R.A.S., J.S., of Bombay, who was enough of a secularist to address, in 1898, the Manhattan Liberal Club on philosophy and religion.[89] In Germany, Frederick the Great was enough of a fellow traveler with atheists that he gave a court position, and refuge, to the atheist Lamettrie.[90] In France, every atheist Jefferson came to know was, as he said, "the most virtuous of men."[91] Atheism is merely an abstention from theological thought and ought to aid, rather than hinder, one engaged in state or government duties.

NULLIFYING WILLS AND TRUSTS

In England, as late as 1850, the common law and prevailing case law caused the nullification by a court of a bequest for:

> . . . best essay on the subject of natural theology, treating it as a science, and demonstrating the truth, harmony, and infallibility of the evidence on which it is founded, and the perfect accordance of such evidence with reason; also demonstrating the adequacy and sufficiency of natural theology, when so treated and taught as a science, to constitute a true, perfect,

and philosophical system of universal religion . . . founded on immutable facts and the works of creation, and beautifully adapted to man's reason and nature, and tending, as other sciences do, but in a higher degree, to improve and elevate his nature and to render him a wise, happy, and exalted being.[92]

The Vice-Chancellor ruled: "I cannot conceive that the bequest in the testator's will is at all consistent with Christianity, and, therefore, it must fail."

In 1745 it was held illegal to make a bequest for "instructing in the Jewish religion," because it "was in contradiction to the Christian religion, which is part of the law of the land."[93]

In 1884 a bequest, without directions, to Charles Bradlaugh and another was nullified simply on proof that the testator *expected* the legatees would use the fund in promoting freethinking.[94] Notwithstanding the repeal in 1913 of a clause in the Act of 1698 which penalized denials of the Trinity, a gift for Unitarianism was held illegal because of its "denial of the Trinity."[95] For a time the validity of a gift for "Christian Science" was in doubt, but the court upheld it on the authority or reasoning of an English decision which legalized a gift for publication of the writings of Joanna Southcote which would include her message that "she was with child by the Holy Ghost, and that a second Shiloh or Messiah was about to be born of her body."[96]

Governors, like judges, would obstruct separation of government from religion. In Ohio, Governors Cox, Davis, and Donahey vetoed legislation accepting a gift of five hundred acres for a natural history preserve. John Bryan, donor, had provided that there would never be any church or religious exercises on the grounds. On May 2, 1923, the legislature repassed the bill over the veto of Donahey.[97]

Daniel Webster's attack on the will of Stephen Girard,

seeking to invalidate the trust for education, makes it of interest to notice the following provisions of Girard's last testament:

> I enjoin and require that no ecclesiastic, missionary, or minister of any sect whatsoever, shall ever hold or exercise any station or duty whatever in the said college; nor shall any such person ever be admitted for any purpose, or as a visitor, within the premises appropriated to the purposes of the said college.
>
> In making this restriction, I do not mean to cast any reflection upon any sect or person whatsoever; but, as there is such a multitude of sects, and such a diversity of opinion amongst them, I desire to keep the tender minds of the orphans who are to derive advantage from this bequest, free from the excitement which clashing doctrines and sectarian controversy are so apt to produce; my desire is, that all the instructors and teachers in the college shall take pains to instill into the minds of the scholars the purest principles of morality, so that, on their entrance into active life, they may, from inclination and habit, evince benevolence towards their fellow-creatures, and a love of truth, sobriety, and industry, adopting at the same time such religious tenets as their matured reason may enable them to prefer.[98]

Supported by opinions of Christian judges of the eighteenth century, Daniel Webster argued that this trust was invalid because:

> The plan of education is derogatory to the Christian religion, tending to weaken men's respect for it and their conviction of its importance. It subverts the only foundation of public morals, and therefore it is mischievous and not desirable.

Theodore Schroeder (1864-1953) bequeathed property for the publication of his writings. A Connecticut court held the trust invalid as "contrary to public policy" because, the judge said, "A reading of the article which he called 'Prenatal Psychisms and Mystical Pantheism' is a truly nauseating experience in the field of pornography."[99] The article was scholarly enough to be [as it was] published in the *International Journal of Psycho-Analysis* (London, 1922). An abstract thereof appeared in *Psycho-analytic Review* (Washington, D.C., 1923). It deserved as much support as was given by the Guggenheim Foundation in 1944 for the project: "An analysis of the mechanism of sex chromosome conjunction during meiosis in male Drosophila." A federal court recognized Schroeder's work in the field of free speech.[100] In *Constitutional Free Speech* (1919) Schroeder reprinted that part of Furneaux's 1770 text on the "ill tendency" test which Jefferson paraphrased in the Preamble to the Bill for Religious Freedom. Schroeder's report on the prosecution of John Asgill (1699-1738) reminds that Jefferson's library had Asgill's speech. The library also had Robert Hall's *Liberty of the Press* (1798).[101] Hall is quoted extensively in Schroeder's *Free Speech Anthology* (1909). So is John Stuart Mill's *On Liberty* (1859). Schroeder's self-education and writings are discussed by Maynard Shipley in *The New Humanist* (Chicago) of March-April, 1933. The Connecticut court could have upheld the Schroeder trust at least as to his works other than the "nauseating" article.

In the course of the Connecticut opinion, O'Sullivan, the judge, said: "The law will not declare a trust valid, when the object of the trust, as the finding discloses, is to distribute articles which *reek of the sewer*."

Schroeder wrote forty-five articles which were published prior to 1910, five of which appeared in the *Albany Law Journal*, three in the *Central Law Journal*, two in the *Blue Grass Blade* (Lexington, Kentucky). Twenty-two magazines took his manuscripts relating to freedom of speech, as if the same did not "reek of the sewer." In his own book he reprinted Milton's *Aeropagitica*, and much from Locke's *Four*

Letters on Toleration, a work which had the approbation of Jefferson, except a passage therein relating to toleration of atheism.

In 1870 the Supreme Court of Pennsylvania upheld a nullification of a bequest to "the Infidel Society of Philadelphia . . . for the free discussion of religion, politics, etc." The court assumed from the name of the Society that it would propagate "denial of the doctrines and obligations of revealed religion." The writer of the opinion further said:

> Indeed, I would go further, and adopt the sentiment and language of Mr. Justice Duncan: "It would prove a nursery of vice, a school of preparation to qualify young men for the gallows and young women for the brothel, and there is not a sceptic of decent manners and good morals who would not consider such a debating club as a common nuisance and disgrace to the city."[102]

The "brothel" is something established and maintained by Christians. Lecky cites the fact that there was a statute of Queen Joanna I in 1347 regulating the houses of ill fame at Avignon, in which, after providing with great detail for the accommodation of the Christians, it was enacted that no Jew shall be admitted, under severe penalties.[103] In 1894 the same court harassed an "Infidel" society in another way. It called The Friendship Liberal League a "religious society" and thereby deprived it of a legacy under a statute invalidating a bequest if made by a testator less than one month before his death. The League was sufficiently religious because it intended "in some way to aid in the social, intellectual, and moral elevation" of its members.[104]

In 1880 the Supreme Court of Pennsylvania declared:

> It may be regarded as settled in Pennsylvania that a court of equity will not enforce a trust where its object is the

propagation of atheism, *infidelity*, immorality or hostility to the existing form of government.[105]

In that state, at that time, a trust for the distribution of Jefferson's *Notes on Virginia* would have been nullified because, according to the Reverend Clement Clarke Moore, it is "a book which contains so much infidelity, conveyed in so insidious a manner, . . ."[106] and, according to the Reverend John M. Mason, contains "affronts to the oracles of God."[107] The Reverend William Linn found in the book "an inexcusable questioning of Scriptural authority."[108]

Wills have been upheld where contested on ground of "insane delusion" and the alleged delusion was religious, because, one judge said, the Bible "has probably been given a wider variety of *interpretations* than any other."[109] The testator disinherited four of his children in supposed obedience to the command in II Thessalonians 3:6 that "ye withdraw yourselves from every brother that walketh disorderly," and the words "and no man gave unto him" (prodigal son) in Luke 15:16.

Courts *do not strike out* religious expressions in a will. J. P. Morgan interpolated a paragraph on his confidence in his own salvation, but a court expunged from the will of Harold O. Binney a paragraph repudiating the first four verses of the Decalogue as "superstitious" and declaring himself "a good infidel."[110]

In England, the decisions were, or would be, consistent with those in America. In 1893 a few members of Parliament supported a bill which provided:

> After the passage of this act, . . . it shall be lawful for any person to create and endow, or create or endow, any trust for inquiry into the foundations and tendencies of religious and ethical beliefs which from time to time prevail, or for the maintenance and propagation of the results of such inquiry.[111]

In 1915, however, a chancery court in England found nothing in the objectives of the Secular Society, Limited, "subversive of morality, contrary to law, or contravening the provisions of any statute." A bequest was held legal.[112] On appeal, the House of Lords, too, found the society and bequest legal.[113]

Paragraph (f) of the Society's memorandum was:

To promote an alteration in the laws concerning religion so that all forms of opinion may have the same legal right of propaganda and endowment.

Paragraph 3(a) read as follows:

To promote, in such ways as may from time to time be determined, the principle that human conduct should be based upon natural knowledge, and not upon supernatural belief, and that human welfare in this world is the proper end of all thought and action.

Lord Sumner of the House of Lords declared:

Experience having proved dangers once thought real to be now negligible, and dangers once very possibly imminent to have now passed away, there is nothing in the general rules as to blasphemy and irreligion, as known to the law, which prevents us from varying their application to the particular circumstances of our time in accordance with that experience. If these considerations are right, and the attitude of the law both civil and criminal towards all religions depends fundamentally on the safety of the state and not on the doctrines or metaphysics of those who profess them, it is not necessary to consider whether or why any given body was relieved by the law at one time or frowned on at another, or to analyse creeds and tenets, Christian and other, in which I can profess no competence. Accordingly I am of opinion that acts merely done in furtherance of paragraph (3)a and other paragraphs of the respondent's memorandum are not now contrary to the law. . . .

COERCIVE ASPECTS OF PRAYERS AND THE BIBLE IN SCHOOLS

A student, Foster North, in 1885 would have completed four years at the University of Illinois, and would have received a degree, but for the fact that forty days before graduation time he was suspended, and denied use of a library, all because he had quietly and without ostentation absented himself from *chapel*. The trustees repeatedly denied reinstatement. The Supreme Court denied relief because he would not offer a "religious" excuse. He was an obscure and indigent *agnostic*, and *all* judges voted against him. But in 1910 a *majority* of the judges ruled in favor of *Catholic* litigants, granting them not only the right of nonattendance at religious exercises in public schools, but also the right to have the ceremonies prohibited. Then, for the first time, the court held that "the free enjoyment of religious worship includes the freedom not to worship." The trustees became willing, in 1914, to grant North his degree if he would attend the commencement exercises, which would begin with "scripture reading and prayer." He refused to attend, but later, according to a newspaper item, the degree was given him, twenty-nine years after completion of the course.[114]

It is coercion or oppression of some kind that brings on suspensions, expulsions, and litigations in school prayer and chapel cases. When the Supreme Court of Illinois finally reversed its anti-agnostic decision, and on behalf of Catholic litigants declared the religious school exercises to be in violation of the Illinois Constitution, it paraphrased a part of Jefferson's Preamble when it declared: "In the very nature of things religion or the duty we owe the Creator is not within the cognizance of the civil magistrate."[115]

The court did not protect from coercion the Catholic parties, but said:

All stand equal before the law, the Protestant, Catholic, Mormon, Mohammedan, the Jew, the Free Thinker, the Atheist.

Whatever may be the view of the majority of the people the court has no right and the majority has no right to force that view upon the minority, however small.

If a pupil is not expelled but merely excused from attending a religious exercise at school, still he may suffer, for the court also said:

> The exclusion of a pupil from this part of the school exercise in which the rest of the school joins, separates him from his fellows, puts him in a class by himself, deprives him of his equality with the other pupils, subjects him to a religious stigma and places him at a disadvantage in the school. . . .

Who gets the "stigma" depends on the faith or prejudices of the majority. A Colorado judge wrote: "We have known many boys to be ridiculed for complying with religious regulations but never one for neglecting them or absenting himself for them."[116]

The absentees are usually "a small minority," and the Wisconsin court said:

> When, as in this case, a small minority of pupils in the public school is excluded, for any cause, from a stated school exercise, particularly when such cause is apparent hostility to the Bible which a majority of the pupils have been taught to revere, from that moment the excluded pupil loses caste with his fellows, and is liable to be regarded with aversion and subjected to reproach and insult.[117]

To the same effect is the following from a Louisiana court:

> And excusing such children on religious grounds, although the number excused might be very small, would be a distinct preference in favor of the religious beliefs of the majority, and would work a discrimination against those who were excused. The exclusion of a pupil under such circumstances puts him in a class by himself; it subjects him to a religious stigma.[118]

The action was brought by two Jews and one Catholic.

The famous *McCollum* case probably arose from the fact that Terry McCollum, aged twelve, suffered because "time and time again his schoolmates tore his clothing, snatched his books and engaged him in fights. . . ."[119] His mother was called an "atheist" by many, but might have had the same case if she were a Jewess, for thirty-five years earlier another "atheist" wrote:

> We can well recall the confusion and mortification of one of our schoolmates of the Jewish faith who was obliged to sit through a long Christmas exercise in which he could not conscientiously join; all the while uncomfortably silent while serving as an object for sideward glances by the rest of the class.[120]

The writer of the foregoing noted, in the same article, that Judge Cooke, who concurred in the 1910 Illinois decision against Bible reading in schools, when again a candidate, was subject to bitter opposition:

> Every effort was thereupon made by religious ranters to prevent his re-election, they having gone the length of issuing circular letters and leaflets calling on all Christians to vote against him.

So judges as well as pupils were subjected to attempted coercions, to which Jefferson would object, for when refusing, as president, to recommend a day of fasting and prayer he wrote:

> . . . it must be meant . . . that this recommendation is to carry some authority, and to be sanctioned by some penalty on those who disregard it; not indeed of fine and imprisonment, but of some degree of proscription, perhaps in public opinion.

And does the change in the nature of the penalty make the recommendation the less a law of conduct for those to whom it is directed?[121]

The matter of coercions in schools was treated by Leo Pfeffer in a statement to a House committee on June 18, 1964. Among the many instances given is that concerning Tom Wall, aged eleven. On advice of his father he refused to repeat the Ten Commandments, and "was punished with a rattan stick, some 3 feet in length and three-eighths of an inch wide, by whipping upon his hand."[122] Coercions were attempted upon adults objecting to the use of the King James versions of the Bible. As to a Father Bapst, "a mob broke into his house, dragged him out, tore off his clothing, tarred and feathered him and, after 2 hours of cruel treatment, finally released him."[123]

Coercion was used even in prisons. A prisoner in the Nebraska penitentiary at Lincoln was punished for refusing to attend chapel service required by a rule of the prison. The Board of Control refused to abrogate the rule. Its opinion, written by Judge Silas A. Holcomb, declared that "the state owes an obligation and a duty" to the prisoners to give them the "benefit of exercises of this sort...."[124]

In a Kansas case a pupil, Philip Billard, was permitted to absent himself during a period of Bible reading. However, he chose to remain but "instead of listening to the reading" he opened his books and pursued his studies. For this he was "suspended." The Supreme Court of Kansas upheld the suspension on the assumption that the various constitutional provisions invoked were not intended to exclude Bible readings because "the noblest ideals of moral character are found in the Bible."[125]

Usually the public and persons affected silently acquiesced in the system of religious observances in tax-supported schools. Woolsey Teller noticed, in 1912, that:

At the United States Naval Academy of Annapolis, Sunday church attendance at the Academy chapel is compulsory on all students, unless a desire is expressed by a cadet to attend a church in town.[126]

Also at that time it was the navy's rule that, "The church pennant is to be hoisted above the ensign during the performance of divine services on board vessels of the navy."

Jefferson's Statute provided that "no man shall be . . . *molested*, or . . . shall otherwise suffer, on account of his religious opinions or belief. . . . Catholics felt "molested" by Protestant services in public schools; and they sued for, and obtained, injunctions. Secularists and sensitive Protestants felt "molested" by the notorious presence of Catholic insignia and garb in Indian schools. For that or other reasons the Commissioner of Indian Affairs, Robert G. Valentine, on January 27, 1912, issued an order that "in government schools all insignia of any denomination must be removed from all public rooms, and members of any religious denomination wearing distinctive garb should leave such garb off while engaged at lay duties as government employees." Catholic dignitaries lodged a *protest* against that order with President William Howard Taft, and on February 4, 1912, President Taft obligingly suspended that order "until such time as will permit a full hearing. . . ."[127] There is no record of any restoration of the order after "hearing." A year later, and elsewhere, it was a Catholic pastor who felt "molested" for the reason, among others, that his school district was using the King James version of the Bible.[128] In 1927, in his own state, Minnesota, a Supreme Court judge remarked that such version is "a Bible whose dedication assails the Pope as the 'man of sin'. . . ."[129]

Often it was a statute that prescribed religious ceremonies in public schools. On March 24, 1916, the New Jersey governor signed the "Iobst bill," which provided for the reading of five verses from the Old Testament at the opening exercises every morning in the public schools. On March 22, 1916, a bill was introduced in the New Jersey Senate to defray "incidental expenses," and one of the items (No. 26) was an appropriation of $59 to the Reverend Harry J. Iobst for accompanying the legislators to a Billy Sunday meeting on February 8th.[130] Billy Sunday's techniques were discussed by H. L. Mencken in the Baltimore *Sun* of March 27, 1916.

In 1922 the same legislature passed a law requiring readings from both the Old and New Testament, and thereupon Jews as well as secularists protested.[131]

In 1916, a Bible-reading bill failed, because of opposition from "promoters of parochial schools."[132] Atheistic parents and pupils would not object, silently conforming to any system and to Jefferson's observation that one half the world are "fools" and the other half "hypocrites" as a result of state and prelatic "coercion."[133] There can be hypocrisy by silence as well as by conforming speech.

Chapter Eleven

JEFFERSON'S TECHNIQUES FOR FREEING NONCONFORMING OPINION AND ARGUMENT

The Preamble to the enacting clauses of Thomas Jefferson's Bill for Establishing Religious Freedom was diplomatic and cautious, and so were the clauses themselves. The first clause proscribed molestation for *"religious opinions or belief."* The deists had religious opinions, and atheists a "belief." If the Bill had used the phrase "religious principles," it would, as later a Massachusetts court said, have had "no reference to atheists."[1]

The second enacting clause grants freedom "by argument to maintain . . . opinions in matters of religion. . . ." Orthodox Christians were conscious of having a "faith" and that it was not acquired by or from "argument." Deism began with, and spread, because of argument. Agnostics and other non-religious people rejected Trinitarian doctrines, and, while their opinions were not religious, they were still "in *matters* of religion."

Fifty years after the passage of the Bill, the clerical historian Francis Lister Hawks complained that the Statute created "an alliance between civil authority and infidelity."[2] Unitarianism was then being denounced as an "infidelity," as was deism.

Jefferson's Bill recited "that to compel a man to furnish contributions of money for the propagation of opinions which he disbelieves and abhors is sinful and tyrannical. . . ." The Assembly expunged, and the Statute omits, the words "and abhors." Jefferson would have preferred retention of them. In his *Notes on Locke*, paraphrasing him, he had written, "I cannot be saved by a worship I disbelieve and abhor." The words "and abhors" were apt. Secularists and Protestant sects, especially the Baptists, abhorred the doctrine of St. Fulgentius that infants dying "without the sacrament of holy baptism . . . must be punished by the eternal torture of undying fire. . . ." Jefferson, and the deists generally, abhorred the doctrines alluded to in his letter wherein he wrote: "It would be more pardonable to believe in no God at all, than to blaspheme Him by the atrocious attributes of Calvin."

A modern, humanitarian, and progressive judge knew, like Jefferson, when to say "abhors," as he did in this passage of his opinion: "I can conceive no more poignant anguish than that of the true father who sees his child, against his will, brought up before his eyes in a religious system which he *abhors*."[3]

The Assembly deleted as a "diabolical scheme"[4] the clause: "that the opinions of men are not the object of civil government, nor under its jurisdiction. . . ." Jefferson restated that principle in *Notes on Virginia*, and in the campaign of 1800 the Reverend Mason denounced it as atheistic.[5]

As drafted, the Preamble began:

> Well aware that the opinions and belief of men depend not on their own will, but follow involuntarily the evidence proposed to their minds. . . .

The Assembly deleted it. Its secularism was evident from absence of the word "faith" and from the common supposition that deistic "opinions" rested on "evidence."

For purpose of argument, Jefferson would paraphrase Locke, as in his note:

> . . . the life and essence of religion consists in the internal persuasion or belief of the mind. External forms of worship, when against our belief, are hypocrisy and impiety.[6]

Jefferson being in Europe, arguments were heard from Madison, mainly on the Assessment Bill.

The second clause of the Preamble to the Bill, as drafted by Jefferson, began thus:

> [Well aware] that Almighty God hath created the mind free, *and manifested his supreme will that free it shall remain by making it altogether insusceptible of restraint....*

The Assembly struck out the words above quoted in *italics*. Why, we do not know, but the language reminds of the heretics burned for refusing to recant nonconforming opinions.

The third clause of the Preamble to the Bill was:

> ... that all attempts to influence it [the mind] by temporal punishments, or burthens, or by civil incapacitations, tend only to beget habits of hypocrisy and meanness, and are a departure from the plan of the holy author of our religion, who being lord both of body and mind, yet chose not to propagate it by coercions on either, as was in his Almighty power to do, *but to extend it by its influence on reason alone....*

The Assembly expunged the clause above *italicized*. It seemed too deistic but, even without it, Jefferson thought of the Statute as "the standard of *reason* at length erected."[7] "Reason" was Jefferson's favorite word when he advised Peter Carr: "Fix *Reason* firmly in her seat," and again when he wrote Waterhouse: "I should as soon undertake to bring the crazy skulls of Bedlam to sound understanding, as inculcate *reason* into that of an Athanasian." In 1784 Ethan Allen published *Reason, the Only Oracle of Man*, and that title expressed his thought; and Paine followed, in 1793, with *Age of Reason*.

The phrase "holy author of our religion" pleased the religionists, the text in Hebrews 12:2 being: "Looking unto Jesus the *author* and finisher of our faith." They sought to add "Jesus Christ" as a prefix to "holy author." Jefferson noticed this in his *Autobiography* where he wrote:

> Where the Preamble declares, that coercion is a departure from the plan of the holy author of our religion, an amendment was proposed, by inserting the word "Jesus Christ," so that it should read, "a departure from the plan of Jesus Christ, the holy author of our religion"; the insertion was rejected by a great majority, in proof that they meant to comprehend, within the mantle of its protection, the Jew and the Gentile, the Christian and Mohametan, the Hindoo, and Infidel of every denomination.

"Denomination" connotes a religious sect, and one could assume that Jefferson meant to protect it, without thinking of secularists, but some clergymen belatedly perceived that Jefferson was not deviating from his purpose to emancipate "*all* men," as evidenced in other clauses. Fifty years later an Episcopalian minister commented:

> . . . and in the spirit of exultation, which he cannot conceal, at the success of his effort to degrade Christianity to a level with the creed of Mecca, he proceeds to relate with approbation a circumstance clearly indicative of his design to heap dishonor upon the faith of Christians. We are informed by him that an amendment was proposed to the Preamble by the insertion of the name of our Saviour before the words "the holy author of our religion," . . . but surely it was not necessary in securing to them such protection, to degrade, not the establishment, *but Christianity itself* to a level with the voluptuousness of Mohammed, or the worship of Juggernaut; and if it be true that there is danger in an established alliance between Christianity and the civil power, let it be remembered that there is another alliance not less fatal to the happiness, and subversive to the intellectual freedom of man—it is an alliance between civil

authority and infidelity; which, whether formally recognized or not, if permitted to exert its influence, direct or indirect, must be found to be equally ruinous in its results. On this subject revolutionary France has once read to the world an impressive lesson, which it is to be hoped will not speedily be forgotten.[8]

William Jennings Bryan in 1904 in a foreword in Volume VIII, Monticello Edition, *Jefferson's Writings*, took the Preamble to mean:

> ... and that if God himself was not willing to use coercion to force man to accept certain religious views, man uninspired and liable to error ought not to use the means that Jehovah would not employ.

That assumed that God was "the holy author" who would not use "coercion," and man "ought not to. . . ." In 1925, however, Bryan was willing that man use the coercion inherent in the anti-evolution statutes.

After the "holy author" clause the Preamble recited:

> ... that the impious presumption of legislators and rulers, civil as well as ecclesiastical, who, being themselves but fallible and uninspired men, have assumed dominion over the faith of others, setting up their own opinions and modes of thinking as the only true and infallible, and as such endeavoring to impose them on others, hath established and maintained false religions over the greatest part of the world and through all time. . . .

The Reverend Mason in *Voice of Warning, etc.* (1800) explains why Jefferson used the pious diction:

> But Mr. Jefferson is not here declaring his *private opinions:* For these we must look to his Notes, which were published *a year after,* and abound with ideas which contradict the au-

thority of the Scriptures. He speaks, in that act, as the organ of an *Assembly professing Christianity;* and it would not only have been a monstrous absurdity, but more than his credit, and the Assembly's too, was worth, to have been disrespectful, *in an official deed,* to that Redeemer whose name they owned, and who was precious to many of their constituents. *Such* Christianity is common with the bitterest enemies of Christ.

The last sentence, above quoted, falsely assumes that Unitarians, deists, and others, not accepting the doctrine of the Trinity, were "enemies of Christ." Christian politicians pretended to think likewise. Hence Jefferson in his Preamble and Madison in his *Remonstrance,* etc., had to keep orthodoxy pacified in the Assembly.

George Mason offered the following for a section in the Virginia Declaration of Rights: "All men are equally entitled to the full and free exercise of religion, according to the dictates of conscience."[9]

Jefferson would protect also all men who abstain from the "exercise." Since the legislators would not recognize secularism, Jefferson could improve on Mason's draft by this: "All persons shall have full and free liberty of religious *opinion;* nor shall any be compelled to frequent or maintain any religious institution."[10] Persons could have an "opinion" without also a "faith."

James Madison, too, saw the necessity of ambiguity to protect the nonreligious when drafting the First Amendment. When the ambiguity finally led to the recognition also of the secularists in the McCollum case, conservative Christians were alarmed, one crying out, "the *infamous* McCollum decision!"[11]

George Mason's phraseology could have encouraged the presentation to the "first republican legislature" of petitions from dissenters to put every religious denomination on an equal footing.[12]

Jefferson in *Notes on Locke* wrote: "Locke denies toleration to those who . . . deny the existence of a god. . . . It was a great thing to go so far . . . but where he stopped short, we may go on."[13] He went "on" in his 1776 Resolution which recited:

> Resolved, . . . that all and every act . . . of the Parliament of England . . . which renders criminal the maintaining of any opinions in matters of religion . . . or which prescribes punishments for the same, ought to be declared henceforth of no validity or force.[14]

One of Jefferson's notes says: ". . . for totally and eternally restraining the civil magistrate from all pretensions of interposing his authority or exercise in matters of religion."[15] His idea was later more clearly expressed in the draft of the Bill where it refers to what is "not the object of civil government."

In the proceedings leading to the adoption, June 12, 1776, of a Declaration of Rights, George Mason drafted a limitation on toleration in these words: ". . . unless under cover of religion any man *disturb the peace*, the happiness or safety of society." That was conforming to an English decision of 1617 which made blasphemy a crime at common law on the supposition that it tended to create a disturbance of the peace.[16]

Madison offered the following substitute:

> . . . and therefore that no man or class of men ought on account of religion to be invested with peculiar emoluments or privileges, nor subjected to any penalties or disabilities, unless under color of religion the preservation of equal liberty and the *existence of the state* be *manifestly* endangered.

That was in coerced conformity to an English decision of 1729 holding that a denial of the miracles of Christ tended "*manifestly* to a dissolution of the civil government."[17]

Jefferson's Preamble and Statute removed limits on toleration.

Supporters of Jefferson's Bill were hampered in pursuing its emancipating objectives because religionists would oppose any obvious removal of governmental powers over "infidels." The passage of the Bill became possible because it purported to be for "religious freedom," and the minority sects needed it. The established church in Virginia was placid, having no heresy hunts or awakenings, and Jefferson noticed: "Our clergy, before the Revolution, having been secured against rivalship by fixed salaries, did not give themselves the trouble of acquiring influence over the people."[18]

The deists, too, were quiescent. Not until 1796 did American clergy become aware of, and incensed against, "infidelity." Thomas Paine's *Age of Reason* had then arrived. While Jefferson's Bill was pending in Virginia, 1779-85, the deists there were not noticed as such, and not until 1857 did a historian report: "Mr. Jefferson, and Wythe, who did not conceal their disbelief in Christianity, took their parts in the duties of vestrymen. . . ."[19] In 1800, of course, some of the clergy were proving Jefferson an "infidel" by quoting from his *Notes on Virginia*.

Of James Madison, Bishop Meade wrote:

> His religious feeling . . . seems to have been short lived. His political associations with those of infidel *principles*, of whom there were many in his day, if they did not actually change his creed, yet subjected him to the general suspicion.[20]

The word "suspicion" connotes "suspect," a term often applied to one suspected of crime, and "suspicion" also means the thought that there is probably something wrong. Obviously Bishop Meade was not extolling Madison. Of the "many" who had "infidel principles" were Edmund Randolph[21] and Charles Cotesworth Pinckney.[22] It was from the library of J. Wales that Jefferson obtained the deistic pamphlets of Thomas Chubb (1679-1747).[23]

Many innovators in theological thought were burned as for "wicked errors," for example, Legate for saying "Christ was not God from everlasting" when the orthodox doctrine was "The Son was begotten from everlasting of the Father." Argument for any alleged "error" was itself punished as blasphemy. Even an orthodox Christian dared not protest against persecutions, but finally Milton could publish his *Areopagitica* (1644), advising "Let her [Truth] and Falsehood grapple." Jefferson abridged Milton's argument when writing this in the Preamble:

> . . . that truth is great and will prevail if left to herself; that she is the proper and sufficient antagonist to error, and has nothing to fear from the conflict unless by human interposition disarmed of her natural weapons, free argument and debate; errors ceasing to be dangerous when it is permitted freely to contradict them.

That was an argument also for peaceful coexistence among the sects, which the Virginia Baptists desired, and needed.

The passage of Jefferson's Bill "failed in successive legislatures from its introduction in June, 1779, until its adoption in January, 1786." What contributed to that adoption, and the defeat of the earlier Assessment Bill, may be inferred from this letter of James Madison to Thomas Jefferson:

> The opposition to the General Assessment gains ground. . . .
> The Presbyterian clergy have at length espoused the side of the opposition, being moved either by a fear of the laity or a jealousy of the Episcopalians. The mutual hatred of these sects has been much inflamed by the late Act incorporating the latter. I am far from being sorry for it, as a coalition between them could alone endanger our religious rights, and a tendency to such an event had been suspected.[24]

Jefferson did not disclose his intent to legalize *all* forms of heterodox speech, or to make it safe "for my neighbor to say there are 20 gods or no God." Knowing well the Christian intolerance that for centuries had imposed martyrdoms on minorities, he thought that it was only while the state government was nascent and free from ecclesiastical pressures that it was possible to get his Bill passed. Accordingly, he wrote in *Notes on Virginia:*

> The shackles, therefore, which shall not be knocked off at the conclusion of this war, will remain on us long, will be made heavier and heavier, till our rights shall revive or expire in a convulsion.

If the Statute had not been passed in 1786, no such emancipating law could have been obtained within the next half century. Religious common law and statutory oppressions long remained in the other colonial states. In Virginia only extra-legal or social persecutions arose, such as the one that Jefferson referred to when writing, in 1820:

> You may have heard of the hue and cry raised from the different pulpits on our appointment of Dr. Cooper, whom they charge with Unitarianism as boldly . . . and as presumptuously as if it were a crime, and one for which, like Servetus, he should be burned.[25]

Chapter Twelve

AFTER FREEDOM IN LAW:
"PUBLIC OPINION" STILL
TYRANNIZED

After abolition of legal penalties upon unbelievers, religionists would continue to think, even to say, that the "infidel" is "odious and detestable" and without "the esteem of mankind."[1] There was notorious antipathy toward Thomas Paine, toward Robert G. Ingersoll in the 1880's, and a few preachers assailed William Howard Taft in 1908.

Jefferson noticed: ". . . the inquisition of public opinion overwhelms in practice the freedom asserted by the laws in theory."[2] In 1824 he wrote:

> You press me to consent to the publication of my sentiments and suppose they might have effect even on sectarian bigotry. But have they not the Gospel? If they hear not that, and the charities it teacheth, neither will they be persuaded. . . . Such is the malignity of religious antipathies that, altho' the *laws* will no longer permit them, with Calvin, to burn those who are not exactly of their creed; they raise the hue and cry of heresy against them, place them under the ban of *public opinion* and shut them out from all the kind affections of society.[3]

In 1793 Colonel John Trumbull at Jefferson's home heard William Branch Giles speak atheistically. So in Trumbull's *Autobiography* appeared this passage:

> In nodding and smiling assent to all the virulence of his friend, Mr. Giles, he [Jefferson] appeared to me to avow most distinctly his entire approbation. From this time my acquaintance with Mr. Jefferson became *cold* and *distant*.[4]

Twenty-three years later Trumbull asked Jefferson for a favor.[5]

To a Jew, Jefferson wrote:

> Your sect by its sufferings has furnished a remarkable proof of the universal spirit of religious intolerance in every sect, disclaimed by all while feeble, and practiced by all when in power. Our laws have applied the only antidote to this vice, protecting all on an equal footing. But more remains to be done, for although we are free by the law, we are not so in practice; public opinion erects itself into an Inquisition, and exercises its offices with as much fanaticism as fans the flames of an *Auto-da-Fe*.[6]

"Fanaticism" rarely arose among the common people, and from them the "infidels" could get respectful attention, which was the very reason for many of the prosecutions for "blasphemy." The speakers were silenced in England, but finally in America Ingersoll was able to say:

> I have made up my mind to say my say. I shall do it kindly, distinctly; but I am going to do it. I know there are thousands of men who substantially agree with me, but who are not in a condition to express their thoughts. They are poor; they are in business; and they know that should they tell their honest thought persons will refuse to patronize them, to trade with them. . . . Every such person is a certificate of the meanness of the community in which he resides. And yet I do not blame these people for not expressing their thought. I say to them: Keep your ideas to yourselves; feed and clothe the ones you love; I will do your talking for you. The church cannot touch, cannot crush, cannot stop me. I will express your thought.[7]

Secularists in politics sometimes expressed their thoughts in papers intended for *posthumous* publication only. *The North American Review* of October, 1907, published the statement of Governor Daniel Henry Chamberlain after his death. The

Denver Post of June 25, 1934, published a statement left by
Senator Charles S. Thomas. Sometimes an "infidel" author
would have some other person take the odium of authorship.
Dr. Thomas Young wrote "a considerable part" of Ethan
Allen's *Reason the Only Oracle of Man.*[8]
In 1749 Lord Chesterfield thought the common people
would think and act only in conformity with prevailing
prejudices. He wrote:

> The herd of mankind can hardly be said to think; their no-
> tions are almost all adoptive; and, in general, I believe it is
> better that it should be so, as such common prejudices con-
> tribute more to order and quiet, than their own separate rea-
> sonings would do, uncultivated and unimproved as they are.
> We have many of those useful prejudices in this country,
> which I should be very sorry to see removed. The good Protes-
> tant conviction, that the Pope is both Antichrist and the Whore
> of Babylon, is a more effectual preservative, in this country,
> against popery, than all the solid and unanswerable arguments
> of Chillingworth.[9]

Jefferson read Chillingworth.[10] The "Whore of Babylon"
propaganda possibly caused the early laws of the Carolinas,
Georgia, New Jersey, and Vermont to bar Catholics from
public office.[11]
When Jefferson sent a copy of his *Syllabus* to Dr. Benjamin Rush, revealing the opinion that Jesus was a human
moralist, the accompanying letter said:

> And in confiding it to you, I know it will not be exposed
> to the malignant perversions of those who make every word
> from me a text for new misrepresentations and calumnies.
> I am moreover averse to the communication of my religious
> tenets to the public; because it would countenance the pre-
> sumption of those who have endeavored to draw before them
> that tribunal, and to seduce *public opinion* to erect itself into

that inquisition over the rights of conscience, which the laws have so justly proscribed.[12]

The tyranny of "public opinion" was again recognized in a letter from Jefferson to Jared Sparks, wherein it was written:

> If the freedom of religion, guaranteed to us by law *in theory*, can ever rise in practice under the overbearing inquisition of public opinion, truth will prevail over fanaticism, and the genuine doctrines of Jesus, so long perverted by His pseudo-priests, will again be restored to their original purity. This reformation will advance with the other improvements of the human mind, but too late for me to witness it.[13]

The temper of some orthodox clergymen, molders of public opinion on necessity for religion, was also noticed by John Adams, for he wrote:

> Oh! Lord! Do you think that Protestant Popedom is annihilated in America? Do you recollect, or have you ever attended to the ecclesiastical strifes in Maryland, Pennsylvania, New York, and every part of New England? What a mercy it is that these people cannot whip, and crop, and pillory, and roast, as yet, in the United States! If they could, they would.[14]

When Lyman Beecher (1775-1863) preached at Litchfield, Connecticut (1810-26) against the "heresy" of Unitarianism, Jefferson had occasion to write that ". . . their [Congregationalists'] sway in New England is indeed Formidable. No mind beyond mediocrity dares there to develop itself. If it does, they excite against it the public opinion which they command, & by little, but incessant and teasing persecutions, drive it from among them. . . ." The letter containing that passage was sent to the editor of the *Richmond Enquirer* "to publish or burn, abridge or alter. . . . Only give it such a title as may lead to no suspicion from whom you receive it. . . .

From contest of every kind I withdraw myself entirely."[15]
In a letter from Jefferson to Dr. Cooper, April 13, 1820,
appear these pertinent phrases:

> The Presbyterian clergy are . . . the most intolerant of all
> sects, the most tyrannical . . . ; ready at the word of the law-
> giver, if such a word could now be obtained, to put the torch
> to the pile. . . . They pant to re-establish, by law, that holy in-
> quisition, which they can now only infuse into *public opinion.*[16]

Jefferson's next sentence was applicable to the clergy of *every*
fundamentalist sect, with respect to the power of inciting
intolerance. He continued:

> We have most unwisely committed to the hierophants of
> our particular superstition, the direction of *public opinion,*
> that lord of the universe. We have given them stated and
> privileged days to collect and catechise us, opportunities of
> delivering their oracles to the people in mass, and of moulding
> their minds as wax in the hollow of their hands.

In a letter from Jefferson to Edward Dowse appears this
sentence:

> We ought with one heart and one hand to hew down the
> daring and dangerous efforts of those who would seduce the
> public opinion to substitute itself into . . . tyranny over re-
> ligious faith.

For centuries preceding the twentieth, a disbelief of one
or more Biblical narratives of miracles made the unbeliever
an "infidel," and, a Connecticut court added, "odious and
detestable."[17] The avowed "atheist" Lamettrie (1709-51)
"was compelled to quit Holland," but he was given sanc-
tuary, and appointed court reader by Frederick the Great in
Berlin.[18] In 1800 Frederick was assailed along with Voltaire

and Jefferson in the Reverend Mason's *Voice of Warning*. Today Frederick is extolled as protector of Freemasonry in Germany and friend of Washington during the Revolution.[19]

In Jefferson's time there was, as he said, a "public" opinion against the heterodox but, after the further spread of Unitarianism, humanism, and indifference, it was the *religious* opinion that harassed dissenters. Even then, elective judges seemed reluctant to make emancipatory decisions, and apologized when making them. Thus, in holding that the dying declaration of an atheist is admissible in evidence, the judge in the case added:

> ... ours is "the land of the free, and the home of the brave" and that though to say "there is no God," both in Scripture and in common knowledge, proves one a fool, and may, for all I know, tie him "to the rocks and clods," yet it does not, and should not, deprive that one of his heritage as a citizen, nor of his standing as one of the "free" and one of the "brave."[20]

In sustaining a motion to quash an information for "blasphemy," after noting that secularists have all the civil rights, the judge said:

> From my earliest recollection, my environment has been such that I cannot refrain from saying that *I regret that this is true*, but the common law offense of blasphemy under the law in this state is not an offense subject to punishment or prosecution.[21]

JOHN STUART MILL
ON THE OATH

. . . two persons, on two separate occasions, were rejected as jurymen, and one of them grossly insulted by the judge and by one of the counsel, because they honestly declared that they had no theological belief; and a third, a foreigner, for the same reason, *was denied justice against a thief.* This refusal of redress took place in virtue of the legal doctrine that no person can be allowed to give evidence in a court of justice, who does not profess belief in a God (any god is sufficient) and in a future state; which is equivalent to declaring such persons to be outlaws, excluded from the protection of the tribunals; who may not only be robbed or assaulted with impunity, if no one but themselves, or persons of similar opinions, be present, but any one else may be robbed or assaulted with impunity if the proof of the fact depends on their evidence. The assumption on which this is grounded, is that the oath is worthless of a person who does not believe in a future state; a proposition which betokens much ignorance of history in those who assent to it (since it is historically true that a large proportion of infidels in all ages have been persons of distinguished integrity and honor); and would be maintained by no one who had the smallest conception how many of the persons in greatest repute with the world, both for virtue and attainments, are well known, at least to their intimates, to be unbelievers. The rule, besides, is suicidal, and cuts away its own foundation. Under pretence that atheists must be liars, it admits the testimony of all atheists who are willing to lie, and rejects only those who brave the obloquy of publicly confessing a detested creed rather than affirm a falsehood. A rule thus self-convicted of absurdity so far as regards its professed purpose, can be kept in force only *as a badge of hatred*, a relic of persecution; a persecution, too, having the peculiarity that the qualification for undergoing it is the being clearly proved not to deserve it. The rule, and the theory it implies, are hardly less insulting to believers than to infidels. For if he who does not believe in a future state necessarily lies, it follows that they who do believe are prevented from lying, if prevented they are, only by the fear of hell. *An Essay on Liberty* (1859).

Appendix B

ROBERT G. INGERSOLL
ON THE OATH

The oath being a religious ceremony, the system of requiring it of witnesses, with no option of making affirmation, would now be a violation of the First Amendment. There is reason for believing that the system actually obstructed rather than aided justice. Colonel Ingersoll, in an interview, expressed himself on this point:

It [the oath] furnishes a falsehood with a letter of credit. It supplies the wolf with sheep's clothing and covers the hands of Jacob with hair. It blows out the light, and in the darkness Leah is taken for Rachel. It puts upon each witness a kind of theological gown. This gown hides the moral rags of the depraved wretch as well as the virtues of the honest man. The oath is a mask that falsehood puts on and for a moment is mistaken for truth. It gives to dishonesty the advantage of solemnity.

The tendency of the oath is to put all testimony on an equality. The obscure rascal and the man of sterling character both "swear," and jurors, who attribute a miraculous quality to the oath, forget the real difference in the men and give about the same weight to the evidence of each because both were "sworn." A scoundrel is delighted with the opportunity of going through a ceremony that gives importance and dignity to his story, that clothes him for the moment with respectability, lends him the appearance of conscience, and gives the ring of true coin to the base metal. To him the oath is a shield. He is in partnership for a moment with God, and people who have no confidence in the witness credit the firm.[1]

Appendix C

FURNEAUX ON THE
"ILL TENDENCY" TEST

Jefferson acquired a copy of the 1771 edition of Philip Furneaux's *Letters to Blackstone.* On the "ill tendency" test Furneaux wrote:

> For if the magistrate be possessed of a power to restrain and punish any principles relating to religion, because of their tendency, and be the judge of that tendency; as he must be, if he be vested with authority to punish on that account; religious liberty is entirely at an end; or, which is the same thing, is under the control, and at the mercy of the magistrate, according as he shall think the tenets in question affect the foundation of moral obligation, or are favorable or unfavorable to religion and morality. But, if the line be drawn between mere religious principle and the tendency of it, on the one hand; and those overt acts which affect the publick peace and order on the other; and if the latter alone be assigned to the jurisdiction of the magistrate, as being guardian of the peace of society in this world, and the former, as interfering only with a future world, be reserved to a man's own conscience, and to God, the only sovereign Lord of conscience; the boundaries between civil power and liberty, in religious matters, are clearly marked and determined; and the latter will not be wider or narrower, or just nothing at all, according to the magistrate's opinion of the good or bad tendency of principles.
>
> If it be objected, that when the tendency of principles is unfavorable to the peace and good order of society, as it may be, it is the magistrate's duty then, and for that reason, to restrain them by penal laws: I reply, that the tendency of principles, though it be unfavorable, is not prejudicial to society, till it issues in some overt acts against the public peace

and order; and when it does, then the magistrate's authority to punish commences; that is, he may punish the *overt acts*, but not the *tendency* which is not *actually* hurtful; and, therefore, his penal laws should be directed against *overt acts only*, which are detrimental to the peace and good order of society, let them spring from what principles they will; and not against principles or the *tendency* of principles.

The distinction between the tendency of principles, and the overt acts arising from them, is, and cannot but be, observed in many cases of a *civil* nature; in order to determine the bounds of the magistrate's power, or at least to limit the exercise of it, in such cases. It would not be difficult to mention customs and manners, as well as principles, which have a tendency unfavorable to society; and which, nevertheless, cannot be restrained by penal laws, except with the total destruction of civil liberty. And here, the magistrate must be content with pointing his penal law against the evil overt acts resulting from them. . . . Punishing a man for the *tendency* of his principles, is punishing him *before* he is guilty, for fear he *should be* guilty.

SYMBOLS FOR TITLES
OF WORKS CITED

A-J L   *The Adams-Jefferson Letters* (University of North Carolina Press, Chapel Hill, 1959).

Bergh   *The Writings of Thomas Jefferson,* Definitive Edition, 20 vols., edited by Albert Ellery Bergh (The Thomas Jefferson Memorial Association of the United States, 1907).

Bonner   Hypatia Bradlaugh Bonner, *Penalties Upon Opinion, or Some Records of the Laws of Heresy and Blasphemy* (Watts & Co., London, 1916).

Catalogue   Catalogue *of the Library of Thomas Jefferson* (Library of Congress, 1953; E. Millicent Sowerby, editor).

Collins and Watts   Collins and Watts, *Biographies of Ancient and Modern Celebrated Freethinkers* (Boston, 1871).

Cousins   Norman Cousins, *In God We Trust* (Harper & Bros., N.Y., 1958).

DNB   *Dictionary of National Biography,* 63 vols. 1885-1900, and 3 supp. vols.

EB   (11th ed.) *Encyclopaedia Britannica* (The Encyclopaedia Britannica Co., N.Y., 1910-1911).

Farrar   Adams Storey Farrar, *A Critical History of Freethought in Reference to the Christian Religion* (D. Appleton & Co., N.Y., 1888).

Foner   Philip Foner, *Basic Writings of Thomas Jefferson* (Citadel Press, N.Y., 1944).

Foote   Henry Wilder Foote, *Thomas Jefferson: Champion of Religious Freedom, Advocate of Christian Morals* (The Beacon Press, Boston, 1947).

Ford   Paul Liecester Ford (Editor), *The Works of Thomas Jefferson* (G. P. Putnam's Sons, N.Y., 1892-99).

Gould   William D. Gould, "The Religious Opinions of Thomas Jefferson," *Mississippi Valley Historical Review,* XX, 191, (Sept., 1933).

Hervey   John, Lord Hervey, *Memoirs of the Reign of George the Second,* 3 vols. (London, 1884); *Memoirs of the Court of George II* (J. W. Croker ed. 1848).

Hollis Christopher Hollis, *The American Heresy* (Minton, Balch & Co., N.Y., 1930).

Kimball Marie Kimball, *Jefferson and the Road to Glory,* 1743-1776 (Coward, McCann, Inc., N.Y., 1943).

Koch G. Adolph Koch, *Republican Religion* (Henry Holt & Co., N.Y., 1933).

L & B *The Writings of Thomas Jefferson,* 20 vols. edited by Lipscomb and Bergh (Washington, D.C., 1903).

Larson Orvin Larson, *American Infidel: Robert G. Ingersoll* (Citadel Press, New York, 1962).

McCabe Joseph McCabe, *A Biographical Dictionary of Ancient, Medieval, and Modern Freethinkers* (Haldeman-Julius Publications, Girard, Kansas, 1948).

McCloy Shelby T. McCloy, *Gibbon's Antagonism to Christianity* (The University of North Carolina Press, 1933).

Macdonald George E. Macdonald, *Fifty Years of Freethought,* 2 vols. (1931).

Malone Dumas Malone, *Jefferson and His Time,* Vol. I (Little, Brown & Co., Boston, 1948).

Meade William Meade, *Old Churches, Ministers and Families of Virginia* (Philadelphia, 1857).

Memoir Memoir, *Correspondence and Miscellanies, From the Papers of Thomas Jefferson,* edited by Thomas Jefferson Randolph (1829).

Mencken Henry L. Mencken, *Treatise on the Gods* (Knopf, N.Y., 1930).

Morais Herbert M. Morais, *Deism in America.*

Morse John T. Morse, *Thomas Jefferson* (American Statesmen Series, 1883).

Padover Saul K. Padover, *The Complete Jefferson* (Tudor Pub. Co., N.Y., 1943).

Papers The Papers of Thomas Jefferson, Julian P. Boyd, Editor (Princeton University Press, 1950-   ).

Parton James Parton, *Life of Thomas Jefferson* (1874).

Pfeffer Leo Pfeffer, *Church, State and Freedom* (The Beacon Press, Boston, 1953).

Pierce   Edward L. Pierce, *Memoir and Letters of Charles Sumner*, 4 vols. (Boston, 1877-1893).

Remsburg   John E. Remsburg, *Six Historic Americans* (The Truth Seeker Co., N.Y.).

Randall   Henry S. Randall, *The Life of Thomas Jefferson*, 3 vols. (N.Y., 1853).

Robertson (1906)   John M. Robertson, *A Short History of Freethought, Ancient and Modern*, 2 vols. (Watts & Co., London, 1906).

Robertson (1929)   *A History of Freethought in the Nineteenth Century*, 2 vols. (Watts & Co., London, 1929).

Robertson (1936)   *A History of Freethought, Ancient and Modern to the Period of the French Revolution*, 2 vols. 4th ed. (Watts & Co., London, 1936).

Schachner   Schachner, *Thomas Jefferson, a Biography*, 2 vols. (Appleton-Century-Crofts, Inc., N.Y., 1951).

Schapiro   J. Selwyn Schapiro, *Condorcet and the Rise of Liberalism* (Harcourt Brace & Co., N.Y., 1934).

Schroeder (1916)   Theodore Schroeder, *Constitutional Free Speech* (1916).

Schroeder (1909)   Theodore Schroeder, *Free Press Anthology* (1909).

Steiner   Franklin Steiner, *The Religious Beliefs of Our Presidents* (Haldeman-Julius Publications, 1936).

Stephen   Sir James Fitzjames Stephen, *A History of the Criminal Law of England* (London, 1883).

Wheless   Joseph Wheless, *Forgery in Christianity* (Knopf, N.Y., 1930).

White   Andrew Dickson White, *A History of the Warfare of Science with Theology in Christendom*, 2 vols. (D. Appleton & Co., N.Y., 1899).

Works   *The Works of John Adams, Second President of the United States* (Little, Brown & Co., Boston, 1856).

NOTES

Chapter One

1. Francis Lister Hawks, *Contributions to the Ecclesiastical History of the United States* (New York, 1836), I, 177–79.
2. *EB*, III, 780.
3. John M. Mason, *Voice of Warning to Christians, etc.* (1800), quoted in Randall, II, Appendix 18. There were insults from "a multitude of pulpits." Randall, II, 570.
4. *EB*, XVI, 129, 130.
5. Ford, IX, 136.
6. TJ to William Carver, Dec. 4, 1823. Ford, XII, 327.
7. TJ to Thomas Law, June 13, 1814. Cousins, 141.
8. *Papers*, XII, 14–18.
9. *Papers*, I, 602–4; Ford, V, 225, 228; Cousins, 121.
10. Ford, V, 151, 152.
11. *McClure v. State*, 9 Tenn. (1 Yerger), 207, 224 (1828).
12. TJ, *Notes on Locke*. Cited in *Papers*, I, 548.
13. *Zorach v. Clausen*, 343 U.S. 306 (April 28, 1952).
14. *U.S. v. Schwimmer*, 279 U.S. 644, where Justice Holmes said: "If there is any principle of the constitution that more imperatively calls for attachment than any other it is the principle of Freethought."
15. *State v. Beal*, 152 S.E. 606, 617. That was the notorious Gastonia, North Carolina, murder case growing out of a strike begun April 1, 1929. At the trial Mrs. Edith Saunders Miller was harassed by this question: "Do you believe in the existence of a Supreme Being who controls the destiny of men, who rewards their virtues or punishes their transgressions here or hereafter?" Mrs. Miller could not legally object, being a witness only and not a party litigant. The Supreme Court of North Carolina did not decide whether it was "error" to permit the question, but decided that, error or not, the question did not harm any of the defendants.

Chapter Two

1. *The King v. Eaton*, Howell's *State Trials*, XXXI, 927.
2. TJ to William Short, Oct. 31, 1819. L & B, XV, 221.
3. Thomas Kelly Cheyne in *EB*, XIV, 364, on *Isaiah*.
4. *The King v. Eaton*, Howell's *State Trials*, XXXI, 927.
5. *Attorney General v. Pearson*, 3 Merivale 353; *Shore v. Wilson*, 9 Clark and Finnelly, 355, 496.
6. Bonner, 99, 100. The will of John Beswick, made June 30, 1879, gave 400 pounds to trustees for Oldham Secular Society. The case was heard in 1903.
7. *EB*, XXVI, 595.
8. Howell's *State Trials*, XXVI, 654. (See *EB*, XXV, 806, for history of editions of *State Trials*.)

9. *Ibid.*

10. *EB*, IX, 341; XXVII, 595.

11. The Reverend Alexander Gordon in *DNB*, XVII, 356–60.

12. Vernon Stauffer, *New England and the Bavarian Illuminati* (Columbia University Press, New York, 1918), 73, 75, 78.

13. Steiner, quoting from appendix to *Reports of Cases, etc.,* by Jefferson. To the same effect is TJ's letter to Thomas Cooper, Feb. 10, 1814. L & B, XIV, 85.

Chapter Three

1. *Bouvier's Law Dictionary* (1897), II, 1238; I, 229.

2. Howell's *State Trials*, VI, 702; Schroeder, 369.

3. *EB*, XXIV, 62.

4. *A–J L*, II, 607.

5. *Com. v. Kneeland*, 20 Pickering 206–20.

6. The Jefferson-Lafayette correspondence on Miss Wright's *A Few Days in Athens* may be found in Ford, III, 324, and L & B, XVIII, 324–28. A biography of Frances Wright has been written by William Randall Waterman, Ph.D.

7. On that case, articles and editorials appeared in *The Truth Seeker* (New York), Feb. 20 and 27, 1926, and March 6, 1926.

8. DELAWARE: *State v. Chandler*, 2 Harrington 553 (1839). In 1881 Judge Comegys sought to have it invoked against Colonel Robert G. Ingersoll. Larson, 161.
CONNECTICUT: Mockus was convicted in the City Court of Waterbury in 1916; and, on appeal to the District Court, a trial resulted in a jury disagreement.
MAINE: *State v. Mockus*, 120 Maine 84.
NEW JERSEY: Prosecution of Charles B. Reynolds in 1886–87, and threats against Colonel Robert G. Ingersoll in 1895. Larson, 161.

9. *Doremus v. Board*, 75 Atl. (2nd) 884 (1960).

10. Statute quoted in 39 *Yale Law Journal* 659 (March, 1930); also in Scharf, *History of Maryland* (1879), I, 174.

11. *EB*, XV, 514.

12. L & B, XV, 425, 427; *A–J L*, II.

13. *Dist. of Columbia v. Robinson*, 30 App. Cas. (D.C.), 283, 12 Ann. Cases 1094 (1908). The Maryland act of 1723 is quoted in *The Truth Seeker*, XXXVII, 435, July 9, 1910, reprinting an article by Mrs. Helen M. Lucas in the Marietta, Ohio, *Daily Times.*

14. *Papers*, I, 530.

15. Atwood's Case, Coke's English King's Bench Reports in the time of James I.

16. Taylor's Case, 3 Keble 607; Ventris, 293.

17. Larson, 202.

18. *EB*, XI, 224b.

19. Schroeder, 272–75; *Journal of the House of Commons*, VI, 539–40, Feb. 20–22, 1650.

20. See title *Asgill* in index to *Catalogue.*

21. Schroeder, 318–22; *DNB*, II, 160–61; *EB*, II, 724.

Chapter Four

1. *EB*, IV, 854.
2. Lecky, *Rationalism in Europe* (1866), II, 113.
3. Bonner, 6, 7, citing Taswell-Langmead, *English Constitutional History.*
4. Bonner, 6; Stephen.
5. *Bouvier's Law Dictionary* (1897), II, 1004.
6. *Papers*, I, 541.
7. Robertson (1936), citing Henry Soames, *Elizabethan Religious History* (1839). The burnings were under the crown's "*supposed* rights of issuing writs for this purpose." *EB*, IV, 854.
8. Howell's *State Trials*, II, 727.
9. *EB*, III, 372.
10. Howell's *State Trials*, II, 727.
11. *Papers*, I, 554.
12. White, II, 304.
13. TJ's note on the margin of page 427, Vol. II, Priestley's *An History*, . . . , in Jefferson's library. TJ wrote: " . . . Yet, says Buchanan, 'I believe the passage to be genuine,' or, in other words, the mystery of the trinity is too important to make ours a craft to be given up." *Catalogue*, II, 188. On the interpolation, see *EB*, XV, 451 note 6, citing Karl Kunstle, *Das Comma Johanneum*. The interpolation is also discussed in Wheless.
14. *EB*, XIII, 551.
15. *American Bar Association Journal*, XXXI, 572, Nov., 1945.
16. *Com. v. Kneeland*, 20 Pickering 220, 236 (1838). See also TJ's note on acts of Parliament in *Papers*, I, 541. *Cf. ibid.*, 530, 531.

Chapter Five

1. TJ to Dr. Cooper, Sept. 10, 1814. L & B, XIV.
2. *EB*, XVII, 111.
3. TJ to Charles Clay, Jan. 29, 1815, L & B, XIV, 182.
4. TJ to William Johnson, June 12, 1823. Bergh, XV, 439, 440.
5. *Ibid.*
6. Adams to TJ, June 22, 1815. L & B, XIV, 332; TJ to Adams, Aug. 10, 1815. L & B, XIV, 343.
7. Adams to TJ, Dec. 3, 1815. L & B, XIV, 14, 17.
8. TJ to Adams. *Memoir*, IV, 205.
9. *De Divinatione*, Book II, par. 24. This book was in Jefferson's library. The title *haruspex* is in *EB*.
10. TJ to William Short, April 13, 1820. L & B, XV, 244.
11. *Papers*, XII, 14–18.
12. TJ to Elbridge Gerry, March 29, 1801. L & B, X, 254.
13. Cousins, 103, quoting Adams to F. A. Van Der Kemp, Feb. 16, 1809.
14. *American International Encyclopedia* (1950), IV, title *Clovis*.
15. *EB*, VI, 563.
16. *State v. Mockus*, 120 Maine Rep. 84, 112 Atl. 39, 14 Am. Law Rep. 871.
17. Cousins, 259.

18. *EB*, V, 358b.

19. Cousins, 262.

20. Henry R. Evans, "Illuminism and Jacobinism in Federal Period of America," *The New Age* (Washington, D.C.), Oct., 1946; Merle Curti, *The Growth of American Thought* (Harper & Bros., New York, 1943), 200. See also Mackey, *Encyclopedia of Freemasonry* (1920), and Stauffer, *op. cit.*

21. Consult Randall, and Charles O. Lerche, Jr., "Jefferson and the Election of 1800 . . . ," *William and Mary Quarterly*, V (Series 3), 473, 474 (1948). The corrected history of the "Goddess" is given by Professor F. A. Aulard in French, and is followed by Charles Downer Hazen in *The French Revolution* (1932), 766.

22. Curti, *op. cit.*, 200.

23. Evans, *op. cit.*

24. Stauffer, *op. cit.;* Ford, IX, 108.

25. " . . . the craft, the power and the profit of the priests." Jefferson to Adams, Aug. 22, 1813. Cousins, 237; Ford, XI, 328; Steiner, 102. "Craft" appears also in TJ's note written on the margin of page 427, Vol. II, Priestley, *op. cit. Catalogue*, II, 121.

26. TJ to Ritchie, January 21, 1816. Ford, XI, 507, 510. This letter is *omitted* in most selections of the writings of Jefferson. Congressman Nelson alleged that the Illuminati sought: (1) Abolition of monarchy and all ordered government; (2) abolition of private property; (3) abolition of inheritance; (4) abolition of patriotism; (5) abolition of the family . . . ; (6) abolition of all religion. Jefferson thought that, according to quotations from Weishaupt as given by Barruel, Weishaupt mainly tried to advocate the doctrine of Perfectibility as taught by Godwin. Jefferson's letter is set out in Stauffer, *op. cit.*

27. Jack Owen, *Skeptics of the Italian Renaissance* (1893), quoting Graymond. Vanini's books in Jefferson's library, see *Catalogue*, II, 17.

28. Thomas Macaulay, *History of England* (1890), V, 226–29.

29. Letter of John Locke, Howell's *State Trials*, XIII, 917–38.

30. Robertson (1936), II, 761.

31. *EB*, IV, 855.

32. Robert H. Vickers, *History of Bohemia* (1894), 605–6.

33. Charlotte Elizabeth, *The English Martyrology* (1843), 105. The book was abridged from the works of John Foxe, and was published in Philadelphia by the Presbyterian Board of Publications.

34. *Liberty* (Washington D.C.), XXVI, No. 4, 102, 115 (1931). As to Askew and Boucher, consult *DNB*.

35. *Frazer's Magazine*, April, 1859; Bonner, 69–71.

36. Ford, I, 483, 485.

37. April 13, 1820. *Memoir*, IV, 320, 322; L & B, XV, 243, 246.

38. Madison to William Bradford, Jr., January 24, 1774, quoted in Cousins, 299. See also "A Crime of Great Magnitude," *Liberty* (Washington, D.C.), May-June, 1967.

39. Howell's *State Trials*, VI, 702–10. See also *DNB*, title *Keach*.

40. As quoted by Lecky, *op. cit.*, I, 362–63, the passage ends with: " . . . must be punished by the eternal torture of undying fire; for although they have commited no sin by their own will, they have nevertheless drawn

with them the condemnation of original sin, by their carnal conception and nativity."
41. Howell's *State Trials*, VI, 702–10.
42. Dr. Joseph Martin Dawson in *Liberty* (Washington, D.C.), XI, No. 2, 8 (1954). See also Joseph T. Buckingham, *Specimens of Newspaper Literature* (Boston, 1850), 167. Passages from Robert Hall's book are given in Schroeder (1909), 31.
43. TJ to Dr. Rush, April 21, 1803. L & B, X, 379, 381.
44. Longacre, "Puritan Justification for Persecution of Quakers," *Liberty* (Washington, D.C.), XXVI, No. 4, 102.
45. TJ in *Notes on Virginia*, quoted in Cousins, 121, 122; Foner, 156.
46. *EB*, XI, 223.
47. William C. Braithwaite, *The Beginnings of Quakerism*, 261.
48. Howell's *State Trials*, V, 801–12; *DNB*, XL, 132.
49. *EB*, XI, 224b.
50. TJ to Lafayette, May 14, 1817. L & B, XV, 114, 116.
51. TJ to John Adams, Aug. 22, 1813. L & B, XIII, 350.

Chapter Six

1. *Updegraph v. Com.*, 11 Sergeant & Rawle's Pennsylvania Reports, 394.
2. *In re Knight's Estate*, 159 Pa. 500, 29 Atl. 303.
3. *The Truth Seeker*, XLI, 648, Oct. 10, 1914.
4. Schroeder (1916), 60–61; *The Truth Seeker*, XLIV, 102, Feb. 17, 1917, and July 21, 1894; *The Truth Seeker Annual* (1895).
5. *Doremus v. Board*, 75 Atl. (2nd) 880, 884 (1960).
6. Larson.
7. MacDonald, I, 414. A history of the case, with names of judges, lawyers, and jurors, is given in the Newark (N.J.) *News*, Jan. 3, 1925, reprinted in *The Truth Seeker*, LII, 40, Jan. 17, 1925.
8. *Peo. v. Ruggles*, 8 Johnson 290.
9. *Rex v. Woolston*, Fitz. 64, cited in notes in 14 Am. Law Rep. 871.
10. *A–J L*, II, 421.
11. *State v. Mockus*, 120 Maine 84, 14 Am. Law Rep. 871.
12. Schroeder (1916), 454; *The Truth Seeker*, Oct. 12, 1918.
13. *The Truth Seeker*, XLI, 580, Sept. 12, 1914.
14. Schroeder (1916), 451; Waukegan *Daily Gazette*, March 3, 1917; *The Truth Seeker*, XLIV, 184, March 24, 1917.
15. *The Truth Seeker*, XLII, 17, citing *North v. Board*, 137 Ill. 296, March, 1891. The school case of 1910 was *Peo. ex rel v. Board*, 245 Ill. 334, 92 N.E. 251.
16. 20 Pickering (Mass.) 206; Robertson (1929), I, 225. Included in notes to 14 Am. Law Rep. 871.
17. Reports of *State Trials* (N.S.), IV, 591. The new series of *State Trials* began to be published in 1888, as explained in *EB*, XXV, 806.
18. Bonner, 37–38; *Annual Register* (1917), 171–74. See title *Hone* in *EB*.
19. *Rex v. Waddington*, 1 Barnewall & Cresswell's English King's Bench Reports, 26; *State Trials* (N.S.), I, 1339.
20. George Jacob Holyoake, *Sixty Years of an Agitator's Life* (1893), Chapters XXVIII, XXX, XXXI.

21. *EB*, V, 339.

22. Robertson (1929), I, 64.

23. *State Trials* (N.S.), IV, 1423; Bonner, 42.

24. The London *Freethinker*, Feb. 8, 1908; *The Truth Seeker*, March 14, 1908; Bonner, 102.

25. Franklin Steiner in *The Truth Seeker*, Feb. 26, 1927.

26. *New York Times*, March 16 and 17, 1927.

27. Third Annual Report of 4-A—1928.

28. *State Trials* (N.S.), I, 1369; Bonner, 49.

29. See index to *Catalogue*.

Chapter Seven

1. *Lawrence v. Smith*, Jacob's English Chancery Reports 471; Eng. Rep. Reprint, XXXVII, 928.

2. Robertson (1929), 121.

3. Harriet Martineau, *History of the Peace* (1877), a history of England during the thirty years' peace, 1816–46. The copyright case does not discuss "immateriality." In a Question Box department of *The Catholic Citizen* in 1928, "immateriality" is recognized as making "body and soul together a single unity. . . ." The dictionary definition is "absence of matter."

4. *Murray v. Benbow*, Section 893, *Joyce on Injunctions*, citing note in Jacob's English Chancery Reports 471.

5. TJ to William Short, Aug. 4, 1820. L & B, XV, 257; Cousins, 153.

6. *Burnet v. Chetwood*, 2 Merivale's English Chancery Reports 441; 35 Eng. Rep. Reprint, 1008. Blount's translation was in Jefferson's library. *Catalogue*, II, 23. So was a copy of the Latin original. *Catalogue*, I, 299.

7. TJ to N. G. Dufief, April 19, 1814. L & B, XIV, 127.

8. *State Trials* (N.S.), IV, 693 ff. The speech for the defense was made by Sir Thomas Noon Talfourd, June 23, 1841, and is reprinted in *The World's Best Orations* (1899), IX, 3569.

9. *EB*, XIX, 864.

10. Lecky, *op. cit.*, II, 118.

11. *EB*, XV, 549.

12. Vickers, *op. cit.*, 655.

13. *EB*, VI, 683.

14. Howell's *State Trials*, VI, 701–10.

15. *St. Hubert Guild v. Quinn*, 118 N.Y. Supp. 582. Proceedings in both the lower and the appellate court are discussed in *The Truth Seeker*, XXXVI, 440, July 10, 1909.

16. Lecky, *op. cit.*, II, 118.

17. Socrates, *The Ecclesiastical History*, Book I, Chapter IX. On Socrates, the historian, and his *History*, consult *EB*, XXV, 338–39.

18. Letter to Peter Carr, Aug. 10, 1787. *Papers*, XII, 14–18.

19. Collins and Watts.

20. Benjamin Franklin, *Autobiography*, Edinburgh ed. (1803), 25. Temple Franklin "made over in politer English" some of the "plain-spokenness." The various editions are mentioned in *EB*, XI, 30.

21. Collins and Watts.

22. Hollis.
23. Adams to TJ, June 22, 1815. L & B, XIV, 322.
24. TJ to Adams, Aug. 10, 1815. L & B, XIV, 343.
25. *EB*, XV, 155.
26. *EB*, XIII, 219.
27. *The Truth Seeker*, Sept. 5, 1908. Letters from New Hampshire library boards are reprinted in *The Truth Seeker*, XXXVI, 21, Jan. 30, 1909. The Ingersoll-Black articles are mentioned in Larson.

Chapter Eight

1. Atwood's Case, Coke's English King's Bench Reports in the time of James I.
2. *State v. Chandler*, 2 Harrington's Reports, 553, 570.
3. TJ to Peter Carr, Aug. 10, 1787. *Papers*, XII, 14–18.
4. *State v. Brandon*, 8 Jones 463, 467 (1862).
5. *Peo. v. Smith*, 263 N.Y. 255, 188 N.E. 746 (1934).
6. *Terminiello v. City of Chicago*, 337, U.S. 1 (1949).
7. TJ to James Smith. *Memoir*, IV, 380.
8. *The Truth Seeker*, XXXVI, 518, August 14, 1909, quoting *The Treasury*.
9. Saul K. Padover, *Democracy, by Thomas Jefferson* (1939), 181.
10. Lord Shaftesbury, *Letter on Enthusiasm* (1708).
11. H. G. Wells, *The Outline of History* (1910–20).
12. Richard Potts in *The Truth Seeker*, March 20, 1915.
13. *EB*, XXI, 407.
14. Cousins, 319, 320.
15. *Rex v. Woolston*, Fitzgibbon's English King's Bench Reports, 64.
16. Schroeder (1916), 339; Bonner, 29, 30; *DNB*, XXVIII, 414.
17. Schroeder (1916), 340; *DNB*, II, 9; Bonner, 30.
18. Howell's *State Trials*, XXXI, 927.
19. Schroeder (1916), 333, 334.
20. *State v. Mockus*, 120 Maine 84.
21. *The Limitation of Toleration, A Discussion between Col. Robert G. Ingersoll, Hon. Frederick R. Coudert, and Ex-Governor Stewart L. Woodford* . . . (The Truth Seeker Co., New York, 1889).
22. " . . . to restrain the profession or propagation of principles on supposition of their *ill tendency* is a dangerous fallacy, which at once destroys all religious liberty . . . [italics author's]."
23. *Lanier v. Lanier*, 5 Heiskell's Tennessee Reports 462.
24. *Rex v. Williams*, Howell's *State Trials*, XXVI, 654–713.
25. *Rex v. Mary Ann Carlile*, Bonner, 44.
26. *State v. Mockus*, 113 Atl. 39.
27. *Law Notes*, 33:165 (Dec., 1929).
28. Am. Bar. Assn. Rep. 51:729 (1926).
29. Charles E. Tuttle in *Century Magazine*, CXV, 1 (Nov., 1927).
30. Joseph N. Ulman in *American Mercury*, XXIV, 95 (May, 1935).
31. C. J. Willes in *Omichund v. Barker*, Willes Reports, 538 (1799).

32. See title *Herod* in *American International Encyclopedia,* VIII (1950).
33. *Wigmore on Evidence,* 2nd ed.
34. *State Trials* (N.S.), IV, 1423.
35. *Updegraph v. Com.,* 11 Serg. & Raele, 394 (1824).
36. *Zeisweiss v. James,* 63 Pa. St. 465 (1870).
37. Macdonald, II, 594.
38. TJ to the Reverend Isaac Story, Dec. 5, 1801. Ford, IX, 320.
39. TJ to Thomas Law, June 13, 1814. Cousins, 141.
40. Adams to TJ, Jan. 22, 1825. *Works,* X, 414–15.
41. *The Truth Seeker,* according to Macdonald, II, 427. The point is that the famous "atheist" became such by his own thinking and without being influenced by any "blasphemous" literature.
42. TJ to Thomas Leiper, Jan. 21, 1809. Cousins, 138.
43. TJ to John Adams, July 5, 1814. Ford, XI, 393, 397.
44. William Adrian Bonger, *Criminality and Economic Conditions;* Cesare Lombroso, *Crime, Its Causes and Remedies;* William T. Root, Jr., *A Psychological and Educational Survey of 1916 Prisoners in the Western Penitentiary of Pennsylvania* (1927).
45. *Federalist,* No. 10.
46. Adams to TJ, Oct. 9, 1787. *Papers,* XII, 221.
47. Howell's *State Trials,* XXVI, 654.
48. *The Complete Works of John M. Mason, D.D.* (1852), IV, 574.
49. Bonner, Appendix B.
50. *EB,* XIII, 358.
51. *The Complete Works of John M. Mason, D.D.* (1852), IV, 574.
52. John Trumbull, *Autobiography* . . . (Yale University Press, New Haven, Connecticut, 1953), 174–75.
53. Root, *op. cit.*
54. *U.S. v. Schwimmer,* 279 U.S. 644, 652 (1929).
55. *Sayings of Cardinal Newman* (1880).
56. *Notes on Virginia.*
57. Irving Dilliard, *One Man's Stand for Freedom* (Knopf, New York, 1963), 410; *In re Anastaplo,* 366 U.S. 82 (April 14, 1961).
58. May 5, 1817. L & B, XV, 108.

Chapter Nine

1. I Ventris 293; 3 Keble 607. *Ventris* is the short title for Ventris's English Common Pleas Reports. Keble reported King's Bench cases during 1661–79.
2. Fitz. 64; Eng. Rep. Reprint 94:655.
3. L & B, XIV, 85.
4. *De Costa v. De Paz,* Ambler's English Chancery Reports 228; Bonner, 29.
5. *EB,* X, 747.
6. *State Trials* (N.S.), IV, 594; Bonner, 57–58.
7. *State Trials* (N.S.), I, 1370; *Annual Register* (1823), 18.
8. TJ to Major Cartwright, June 5, 1824. L & B, XVI, 42, 51.
9. To James Smith, Dec. 8, 1822. L & B, XV, 408, 409.

Chapter Ten

1. *Jackson v. Gridley*, 18 Johnson 93, 103.
2. Willes Reports, p. 538 (1799).
3. Mr. Justice Dawson of the Supreme Court of Kansas. Am. Bar Assn. Rep. 26:778 (1926).
4. *Shaw v. Moore*, 49 N.C. (4 Jones L.) 25.
5. *State v. Pitt*, 166 N.C. 268, 271 (1914).
6. *Jones v. Harris*, 1 Strobhart's S.C.L.R. 163 (1846); *State v. Abercrombie*, 130 S.C. 358 (1924).
7. Constitution of 1867. Quoted in *The Truth Seeker*, LVI, 629, Oct. 5, 1929.
8. TJ to John Adams, May 5, 1817. *A–J L*, II, 512.
9. *Atwood v. Welton*, 7 Conn. 66, 70.
10. *Quarterly Christian Spectator*, Sept., 1829.
11. *Curtiss v. Strong*, 4 Day 52.
12. *Central, etc., R. Co. v. Rockafeoow*, 17 Ill. 543.
13. *Hairn v. Bridalut*, 37 Miss. 209, citing Calvin's Case, 7 Coke's English King's Bench Reports, 17b, 77. Eng. Rep. Reprint 397.
14. *Thurston v. Whitney*, 2 Cushing 104.
15. *Peo. v. Most*, 128 N.Y. 108, 27 N.E. 970 (1891).
16. *Odell v. Koppee*, 5 Heiskell 88 (1871).
17. At trial of Lady Alice Lisle (1685); *Wigmore on Evidence*, 2nd ed.
18. *Jordan v. Smith*, 14 Ohio 199, 202 (1846).
19. Monroe to TJ, May 25, 1800. *The Writings of James Monroe* (New York, 1903), III, 180.
20. Perry's Case, 3 Grattan (44 Va.), 632, 644. The "proscribed man" may suffer in various other ways. If a confession is ascribed to him, he cannot deny it, and he is also barred from proving that an alleged confession was false, or obtained by threats, force, or torture.
21. *The Quarterly Christian Spectator* (New Haven, Connecticut), Sept., 1829.
22. A new item of Dec. 4, 1929, quoted in *The Truth Seeker*, Dec. 21, 1929, in an editorial not disapproving the offered waiver but objecting to the favoring of only *one* class, the priesthood. The judge was Moscowitz and the witness was Father Duffy.
23. The verbose Sixth Chapter of The Confession of Faith of the New England Churches was quoted, at least in part, in one of the opinions in *Hale v. Everett*, 53 New Hampshire 9, where also is a reference to Baird, *Religion in America* (1856), wherein the requirement of the oath proves this country to be "Christian."
24. *U.S. v. Lee*, Fed. Cases, No. 13, 586.
25. *Gillars v. U.S.*, 182 Fed. (2nd) 962, 969 (1950).
26. *The Debunker* (Girard, Kansas), Feb., 1931.
27. *EB*, XIX, 943; John Edwin McGee, *A History of the British Secular Movement* (Haldeman-Julius Publications, Girard, Kansas, 1948), 66. The movement leading to the passage of the Oaths Act was discussed in *National Reformer* (London) during the period from Dec. 26, 1886, to Jan. 20, 1889.
28. *Clinton v. the State*, 33 Ohio State, 27, 33 (1877).
29. J. Crawford Biggs, "Religious Belief as Qualification of a Witness,"

The North Carolina Law Review, VIII, No. 1, 30, 35, Dec., 1929. He quotes with approval a sentence from *Greenleaf on Evidence* to the effect that a law excluding atheists "is both unjust and unpolitic [p. 37]."

30. Statutes of Nebraska and Iowa.

31. *Wigmore on Evidence,* 2nd ed.

32. *Maden v. Catanach,* 7 Huristone and Norman's English Exchequer Reports 360; reprint 158:512.

33. *Quarterly Christian Spectator,* Sept., 1829.

34. *Norton v. Ladd,* 4 N.H. 444 (1828).

35. Minneapolis *Daily News,* Oct. 19, 1929, as quoted in *The Truth Seeker,* p. 717, Nov. 9, 1929. Quoted at p. 709 is an article which had appeared in *The Nation.* The opinion of the North Carolina Supreme Court in the Gastonia, North Carolina, murder case was published in *State v. Beal,* 199 N.C. 278.

36. New York *Evening Journal,* June 20, 1913; *The Truth Seeker,* XLII, 419, July 5, 1913.

37. *Commonwealth v. Buzzell,* 16 Pickering 153 (Mass., 1834).

38. F. M. Holland, lecture of March 1, 1885 (J. P. Mendum, Boston, 1885).

39. *Peo. v. Most,* 128 N.Y. 108, 27 N.E. 970. On John Most, see that title in *EB.*

40. *Brink v. Stratton,* 176 N.Y. 150, 68 N.E. 148. Quoting from the *New York Herald Tribune, The Truth Seeker* of Nov. 2, 1929, said: "Since a ruling of the Court of Appeals in 1903 . . . our law has been both generous and clear." The court did not actually so rule, but it has since respected the separate opinion of Judge Edgar M. Cullen.

41. Act of April 23, 1909. On Palmer, see Macdonald, II, 263.

42. *Donnelly v. State,* 26 N.J.L. 463, 601.

43. *State v. Rozell,* 279 S.W. 705, 712.

44. *Carver v. U.S.,* 164 U.S. 694, 697 (1897). See also *U.S. Law Review,* LXVI, 192 (April, 1932).

45. *Gambrell v. State,* 92 Miss. 728, 46 So. 138, 17 L.R.A. (N.S.), 291; 16 Ann. Cases (1906), 147.

46. *The Truth Seeker,* XXXV, 308, May 16, 1908.

47. *Rex v. Pike,* 3 Carrington and Payne's English Nisi Prius Reports 598 (1829).

48. *Goodall v. State,* 1 Or. 333.

49. 24 *Harvard Law Review* 485, April, 1911.

50. *Stow v. Converse,* 3 Conn. 325, 342 (1820).

51. Harry Elmer Barnes, *Battling the Crime Wave* (1931). *Cf. Journal of Criminal Law and Criminology,* XX, 489 (Feb., 1930).

52. J. Madison Watson, *Independent Fourth Reader* (1878).

53. *Jones v. State,* 145 Ala. 51, 40 So. Rep. 947.

54. *Rex v. Pike,* 3 Carrington and Payne's English Nisi Prius Reports 598 (1829).

55. *McKelton v. State,* 88 Ala. 181, 7 So. 38.

56. *McGuff v. State,* 88 Ala. 147, 7 So. 35 (1889).

57. *State v. Williams,* 111 La. 179, 35 So. 505 (1904).

58. *Shelley v. Westbrooke,* Jacob 266; Bonner, 36.

59. *In re Besant,* 11 Law Reports (Chancery Div.) 508; Bonner, 81. The works of Annie Besant are included in McGee *op. cit.*

60. Larson.
61. *Notes on Virginia*, L & B, XII, xv; Cousins, 123.
62. *Maxey v. Bell*, 41 Georgia 184.
63. Letter of Hughes in *The Truth Seeker*, LII, 292, May 9, 1925.
64. TJ to George Ticknor, May, 1817. Ford, XII, 60. TJ to Albert Gallatin, June 16, 1817. Ford, XII, 73.
65. *Eaton v. Eaton*, 191 Atlantic 839 (1937); *Harvard Law Review*, XL, 831; *New York Times*, Jan. 20, 1936; *Rocky Mountain News* (Denver, Colorado), Feb. 7, 1936.
66. *Stow v. Converse*, 3 Conn. 325.
67. Parton, 211, 212; *Notes on Virginia*; Steiner.
68. Butte *Miner*, as quoted in *The Truth Seeker*, XLIII, 185, March 18, 1916.
69. *Attorney General v. Bradlaugh*, 14 Law Reports (1885) 667; Hypatia Bradlaugh Bonner, *Charles Bradlaugh* (1894).
70. *Papers*, I, 530.
71. *Wright v. State*, 24 Ala. App. 378 (1931).
72. *State v. Pitt*, 166 N.C. 271, 80 S.E. 1060 (1914).
73. *McClure v. State*, 9 Tenn. (1 Yerger) 207 (1829). Constitutions of Arkansas and Mississippi are the same with the exception of the "future state" clause.
74. *State v. Levy*, 187 N.C. 581. See also *North Carolina Law Review*, VIII, 31, 35.
75. The oath is quoted by J. Brewer in *Holy Trinity Church v. U.S.*, 143 U.S. 457 (1892). The Delaware Constitution of 1897 provides (Art. I, Sec. 2) that "no religious test shall be required."
76. *Torcaso v. Watkins*, 367 U.S. 488; 81 Sup. Ct. 1680.
77. TJ to John Adams, May 5, 1817. *A–J L*, II, 512.
78. *Stow v. Converse*, 3 Conn. 325, 342.
79. *Quarterly Christian Spectator*, Sept., 1829.
80. *EB*, I, 53.
81. Robertson (1929), I, 121.
82. In *Gathered Sheaves*.
83. *The Truth Seeker*, Sept. 5, 1908, quoting the Louisville *Courier*.
84. Under the title *Papists, Bouvier's Law Dictionary* defines the term "papists" and cites the later emancipating and repealing statutes, e.g., Act of 10 Geo. IV, c. 7.
85. Miriam Allen DeFord, *The Truth Seeker*, LVII, 11, Jan., 1930.
86. *The Truth Seeker*, LI, 104, Feb. 16, 1924.
87. For example, Dr. A. Wakefield Slaten was dismissed in 1912 from the Department of Biblical Literature at William Jewell College, Liberty, Missouri. Dr. Horace Calvin Day at Howard College "was requested to resign" for nonbelief in the "whale" and "ark" stories, as reported in *Literary Digest*, p. 22, Jan. 4, 1930. In 1923 at Fort Sumner, New Mexico, the superintendent of schools was dismissed for teaching "evolution"; and he produced Woodrow Wilson's letter approving "organic evolution."
88. Schenectady *Gazette*, April 4, 1916, as quoted in *The Truth Seeker*, XLIII, 275, April 29, 1916.
89. Macdonald, II, 170.
90. *EB*, title *Lamettrie*.
91. TJ to Thomas Law, June 13, 1814. Cousins, 141.

92. *Briggs v. Hartley,* 19 L.J.Ch. Cas. 416. Reviewed in Bonner, 68; criticized in *Bowman v. Secular Society,* Appeal Cases, 406 (1917).

93. *Da Costa v. De Paz,* Ambler, 238. The fund was ordered diverted to a foundling hospital. *In re Bedford Charity,* 2 Swanston, 532.

94. Bonner, 97; 57 Law Times Reports (N.S.) 519; *National Reformer,* 58, 104, 108, 298 (1887).

95. *Attorney General v. Pearson,* 3 Merivale 353; *Shore v. Wilson,* 9 Clark & Finnelly, 355, 495, 8 Reprint 450, 507, 531 (argument of counsel).

96. *Glover v. Baker,* 76 N.E. 393, 85 Atl. 916 (1912), following *Thornton v. Howe,* 31 Beavan's English Rolls Court Reports 14; 54 Eng. Rep. Reprint 1042.

97. Macdonald, II, 581.

98. *Vidal v. Girard's Executors,* 2 How. (U.S.) 126 (1844).

99. *The Fidelity Title & Trust Co. v. Clyde, et al.,* 143 Conn. 247 (1956).

100. *C.I.O. v. Hague,* 25 Fed. Supp. 127, 136.

101. *Catalogue,* III, 135.

102. *Zeisweiss v. James,* 63 Pa. State 465.

103. Lecky, *op. cit.,* I, 265.

104. *In re Knight's Estate,* 159 Pa. 500.

105. *Manners v. Library Company,* 93 Pa. St. 465.

106. Clement Clarke Moore, *Observations* . . . (1804).

107. Mason, *op. cit.* The pamphlet was reprinted in full, with notes, in Vol. IV of *The Complete Works of John M. Mason, D.D.*

108. Gould, 192.

109. *In re Elston's Estate,* 262 Pac. (2nd) 148 (Okla., Oct. 13, 1953).

110. Surrogate Court, New York. Quoted in *The Truth Seeker,* XLII, 245, April 17, 1915.

111. Charles Watts, Birmingham, England, in *The Truth Seeker,* p. 23, January 13, 1894.

112. *In re Bowman,* 2 Chancery 447 (1915), Annotated Cases 1917B 1017.

113. *Bowman v. Secular Society, Ltd.* Appeal Cases 406 (1917), Annotated Cases 1917D 751, noted in *Harvard Law Review,* XXXI, 289, 291 (Dec., 1917).

114. *Detroit Tribune,* June 21, 1914, as quoted in *The Truth Seeker,* LIII, 404, June 26, 1926. When Mr. North first tried to obtain reinstatement, the governor of the state had ordered that convicts in the penitentiary not be compelled to attend chapel exercises.

115. *Peo. ex rel v. Board of Education,* 245 Ill. 334, 92 N.E. 25 (1910). The story of Mr. North is given in *The Truth Seeker,* XLII, 17, January 9, 1915. It cites 137 Ill. Rep. 296, as the case involving North. The opinion in the later (1910) case was followed by the dissenting judge in *Wade v. State of Ohio,* May 29, 1928.

116. *Peo. ex rel. v. Stanley,* 81 Colo. 276, 255 Pac. 610 (1927).

117. *State v. District Board,* 76 Wis. 177, 44 N.W. 967; 7 L.R.A. 330; 10 Am. Rep. 41. While the controversy was between Protestants and Catholics at Edgerton, Wisconsin, the decision was gratifying to rationalists. *Cf. The Truth Seeker,* July 5, 1890.

118. *Herold v. Parish Board,* 68 Southern Rep. 116. Comment on the case when it was still in the trial court was made in *The Truth Seeker,* Nov. 8, 1913, with a quotation from the Catholic Boston *Pilot.*

119. From a letter by Terry's grandfather in the Rochester, New York,

Times-Union, Feb. 19, 1947. Quoted in *The Truth Seeker*, LXXIV, 90, May, 1947.

120. Woolsey Teller in *The Truth Seeker*, XXXIX, 705, Nov. 9, 1912, citing (as to Judge Cooke) *America*, p. 279, June 29, 1912.

121. TJ to the Reverend Samuel Miller, *Memoir*, IV, 103.

122. *Congressional Record*, June 18, 1964; *The Liberal* (Philadelphia), XVIII, No. 11, 2.

123. *Ibid.*

124. *The Truth Seeker*, XLI, 136, Feb. 28, 1914; Lincoln *Daily News*, Feb. 11, 1914.

125. *The Truth Seeker*, XXXVII, 289, May 7, 1910, quoting the Topeka *Daily Capital*, and an opinion of the Supreme Court rendered in April, 1904. J. B. Billard, the father, was elected mayor of Topeka, April 4, 1910.

126. *The Truth Seeker*, Nov. 16, 1912, citing Park Benjamin, *The United States Naval Academy*, pp. 379–80.

127. Washington *Herald*, April 8, 1912; *The Truth Seeker*, XXXIX, 244, April 20, 1912.

128. Minneapolis *Journal*, April 17, 1913; *The Truth Seeker*, XL, 280, May 3, 1913.

129. *Kaplan v. School Dist.*, 171 Minn. 142, 214 N.W. 18, 57 A.L.R. 185 (1927). The "dedication" was an epistle to King James I, and was printed in a preface to the Bible prior to the time of later revisions.

130. *The Truth Seeker*, XLIII, 228, 233.

131. Macdonald, II, 559.

132. *The Truth Seeker*, XLIII, 261, April 22, 1916.

133. *Notes on Virginia.*

Chapter Eleven

1. *Thurston v. Whitney*, 56 Mass (2 Cushing) 104.

2. Hawks, *op. cit.*, I, 177–79.

3. *In re Doyle*, 16 Mo. App. 159, 166 (1884).

4. Ford, II, 438n.

5. Randall, III, Appendix 18.

6. *Papers*, XII, 14.

7. *Papers*, I, 602–4; Cousins, 121.

8. Hawks, *op. cit.*, I, 177–79.

9. Charles Ramsdell Lingley, *The Transition in Virginia* . . . (1910), 166.

10. *Papers*, I, 363.

11. *American Bar Association Journal*, XXXIV, 817.

12. *Papers*, I, 526.

13. *Ibid.*, 548.

14. *Ibid.*, 530.

15. *Ibid.*, 531.

16. Atwood's Case, Coke's English King's Bench Reports in the time of James I.

17. *Rex v. Woolston*, Fitzgibbon's English King's Bench Reports. Madison's language is quoted in the 1901 *Annual Report of American Historical Association*, I, 163.

18. TJ to John Adams, Oct. 28, 1813. *A–J L*, II, 387, 389.

19. Meade, 191; Foote, 6.
20. Meade, 100.
21. Moncure Daniel Conway, *Omitted Chapters of History Disclosed in the Life and Papers of Edmund Randolph* (1888), 156.
22. Herbert M. Morais, *Deism in America*. It was this Pinckney who said, "Millions for defense, but not one cent for tribute." *EB*, XXI, 617.
23. *Catalogue*, II, 22n. "Though he acquired little renown in England he was regarded by Voltaire and others as among the most logical of the deist school." *EB*, VI, 322. Many of his works appeared posthumously (1748), and prosecution for blasphemy was precluded. Chubb is noticed by Farrar, 142.
24. Madison to TJ, Aug. 20, 1785. Cousins, 308.
25. TJ to Robert Taylor, May 16, 1820. L & B, XV, 252, 254.

Chapter Twelve

1. *Stow v. Converse*, 3 Conn. 325, 342 (1820).
2. TJ to Adams, January 22, 1822. L & B, XV, 308.
3. TJ to George Thatcher, January 26, 1824. Ford, XII, 332.
4. Trumbull, *op. cit.*, 174, 175.
5. Trumbull to TJ, Dec. 26, 1816.
6. TJ to James Barbour, January 19, 1817. L & B, 242.
7. Robert G. Ingersoll, *Liberty of Man, Woman and Child* (1877).
8. Curti, *op. cit.*, 157.
9. Letter, CLXXVI, Feb. 7, 1749.
10. *Papers*, I, 553, 553n.
11. As to the laws, see "Surviving Religious Test," *St. Louis Law Review*, XVIII, 105, Feb., 1933.
12. April 21, 1803. Ford, IX, 457; *Memoir*, III, 506; Cousins, 168.
13. Nov. 4, 1820. Bergh, XV, 288; Cousins, 156.
14. Adams to TJ, May 18, 1817. L & B, XV, 118.
15. TJ to Thomas Ritchie, Jan. 21, 1816. Ford, XI, 510. The proposed letter was addressed to Horatio Gates Spafford and was dated Jan. 10, 1816.
16. Cousins, 150; *Memoir*, IV, 322; Bergh, XV, 243.
17. *Stow v. Converse*, 3 Conn. 225.
18. *EB*, XVI, 129, 130.
19. William C. Blaine in *Scottish Rite Journal* (St. Paul, Minnesota), Dec., 1967.
20. Rice, J., in *Wright v. State*, 135 Southern Rep. 736–38 (1931).
21. Waukegan (Illinois) *Daily Gazette*, March 3, 1917; Schroeder (1916), 453.

Appendix B

[1] Colonel Ingersoll. Interview with Charles Watts, of London. Truth Seeker Tracts, New Series. No. 41, pp. 759–60.